KU-158-050

# Multimedia

# Multimedia

## Neil Fawcett

Hodder & Stoughton

A MEMBER OF THE HODDER HEADLINE GROUP

A catalogue record for this title is available from the British Library

ISBN 0 340 60902 8

First published 1994
Impression number     11  10  9  8  7  6  5  4  3  2
Year                         1999  1998  1997  1996  1995

Copyright © 1994 Neil Fawcett

Typeset by Multiplex Techniques Ltd, Orpington, Kent.
Printed in Great Britain for Hodder & Stoughton Educational, a division of Hodder Headline Plc, 338 Euston Road, London NW1 3BH by Cox & Wyman Ltd, Reading, Berkshire.

# CONTENTS

# – ACKNOWLEDGEMENTS –

A number of products are referred to in this book. The names of such products may be registered trademarks and are acknowledged as being the property of their owners. As many trademarks and owners as possible are listed below.

Adlib
Adobe: Premiere
Aldus
American Mega Trends International (AMI)
Apple: Macintosh, System 7.0 and QuickTime
Apricot: Xen-;LS II
Asymmetrix: Toolbook
Atari: ST and 800XL
Autodesk
Commodore: Amiga 500
Creative Technology: Soundblaster, Soundblaster Pro
Fast Electronics: Movie Machine
Gold Disk: Animation Works Interactive
Guildsoft
Hitachi
IBM: OS/2, Microchannel Architecture, AIX
Intel: Pentium, Indeo, SmartVideo
Iterated Systems: Images III, Colorbox
Knowledgeware
Kodak: Photo CD
Lotus: 1-2-3
Macromind: Action!
Media Vision
Microsoft: MS-DOS, Windows, Word, PowerPoint, Excel, Dinosaurs, Encarta, Video for Windows
Mitsubishi: M1000
NEC: MultiSpin and TripleSpin
Novell: Netware
Panasonic
Philips: Matchline

Samsung: SyncMaster 5C
Screen Machine: Video Machine Lite
Software Toolworks
Sony
Sound System 2.0, Windows NT
Toshiba
VideoLogic: 928Movie, Captivator, Media Vision
Weitek: Power 9000
Wordperfect: Wordperfect
Wordstar
Xerox
Yamaha

During the research and writing of this book I was fortunate to have had the help of many people. Firstly, I would like to thank my 'better half' Alison for putting up with many late nights and bad moods, and then to the staff of *Computer Weekly* for all their help.

Richard Topping, Sophie Brooks and other staff at Text 100 who work on the Microsoft account were invaluable in the creation of *Teach Yourself Multimedia*. I would also like to thank Samsung's UK General Manager Ali Demin and Apricot's marketing communications manager James Blackledge for the use of their PCs and also Phil of Intel.

UK software and hardware suppliers Datrontech and Guildsoft were very forthcoming in their supply of CD-based software and video cards. Thank you.

And finally, a big thank-you to Dave Mackin [Editor of *Teach Yourself Multimedia*] for taking the prolixity of a news journalist and turning it into a book!

# 1
# WHAT IS MULTIMEDIA?

What is multimedia? The object of this book is to answer this question from both the technical and business points of views. Multimedia is an open book that is both stimulating and full of significant business opportunities. But most important to you as a reader is the fact that multimedia can be fun and entertaining.

Historically multimedia is not a new thing. The mixing of MULTIple MEDIA (hence multimedia), such as stereo sound, still images, text and motion video sources, has been performed for many years by people in the computer industry.

IBM, the biggest maker of computers in the world, has dabbled in mixing images on computer for many years, and now with its latest operating system, OS/2 Version 2.1, the company is selling a powerful development environment for multimedia. However, OS/2 is not the most popular operating system for developing multimedia software despite its powerful design.

Multimedia builds on the simple fact that from birth we all learn from a combination of sound and pictures. At school we learn to read and write from teachers building a relationship between pictures and words. Given enough exposure to this a child will learn a vocabulary, and the whole idea of multimedia builds on this technique. Why waste a 100 words describing how a building looks when a single picture will say what 1000 words cannot ever describe. The picture of a child crying tells a message immediately, whereas words can be misunderstood. Audio also has a similar teaching ability and when combined with a picture, especially a moving picture (video), the learning experience is enhanced and becomes more enjoyable.

Speech is an important part of learning and when combined with still images and video images it also becomes a powerful teaching tool. Through the use of multimedia, the true power of all these different data types, which the computer industry has now dubbed 'rich data types', is that anybody can take advantage of an exciting new kind of teaching, selling or business presentation tool.

# — The development of multimedia —

The personal computer (PC) was launched in 1981 when IBM collaborated with two companies Intel and Microsoft. For its part IBM was protecting its position in the computer industry and Intel and Microsoft simply wanted to break into an emerging marketplace. In Chapter 5 we will take a detailed look at the hardware characteristics of the IBM compatible PC.

Today the IBM PC, which has been cloned by hundreds of other computer makers, is the *de facto* standard on the majority of desktops around the world. Market research companies estimate that there are as many as 100 million PCs in use around the world. Since its launch in 1981 the PC has changed quite significantly in terms of power and its capability to handle rich data types in addition to the minimal text and numeric data associated with spreadsheet and word processing applications.

Although some elements of multimedia have existed for a number of years, what makes a significant difference now is that multimedia has become an affordable technology. Everybody from the poorest student to the richest large business can readily afford the basic components that come together to create multimedia. Added to this is the arrival of much sought after standards.

If you dissect the word multimedia you end up with two chunks: multi and media. The first part refers to the 'multiple' pieces that can go together to create the technology. The second element 'media' refers to the individual ways of providing information, such as sound, video (be it from a television or a camera), still images or animation, and music. But owning these separate pieces is not enough. Multimedia truly comes to life when you can mix and interact with these different elements.

Many computers in the UK, such as the Commodore Amiga or Atari ST are commonly referred to as 'games' machines. But these machines have the two core components of multimedia – sound and graphics – inherent to their design.

Any user group meeting concerned with these computers will have a number of 'demo' disks on offer that show how the stereo sound capability of the Amiga or ST mixed with graphics animations can bring the computer to life. The quality of much of this 'demo' software is very good, with many hours of programming undertaken by programmers who have a detailed knowledge of these computers.

However, multimedia is not about programming. It should not, and indeed does not, need a professional programmer to create software that uses motion video and stereo sound as its basis. To meet this demand the software community has now rallied around the IBM compatible computer to deliver a common platform for multimedia software development. Historically, though, this has not always been the case.

Many will know the PC as a business computer for word processing or spreadsheet work. Until recently, few thought of it as a computer for games or multimedia software. This certainly has been the case for the IBM PC and the myriad of companies who have copied or cloned the original design.

When the PC first appeared in 1981 it was a simple tool that was pushed to deliver adequate word processing and spreadsheet analysis. In 1994 this is quite simply not the case.

The original IBM PC was based around a microprocessor – a silicon brain that controls the computer's every action – called the 8086/88 which was designed and manufactured by the company Intel. The 8086/88 is an 8-bit chip, which means it processes data 8 bits (pieces) at a time, and it delivers a very basic level of performance. In 1981 the thought of using such a PC to process video images and sound would have been crazy.

However, Intel has continued to innovate in the area of microprocessor chips with the launch of the 16-bit 80286 chip, 32-bit 80386, 32-bit i486 and the latest silicon chip in its product family the 64-bit Pentium microprocessor. As these chips have appeared they have increased dramatically in power. The 80386 chip was the first chip from Intel that could really cater for multimedia. Although the 80386 arrived in 1986 the rest of the computer industry, and in particular the software companies, were not ready for it. Software writers had enough problems creating a suitable operating system to replace the antique 8/16-bit Disc Operating System (MS-DOS) software that sits on top of an Intel chip and allows it to run software like WordPerfect and Lotus 1-2-3.

In its own right the 80386 chip is powerful and capable of manipulating video, sound and animations. Two years before the 80386 chip was introduced, Microsoft launched some software called Windows. Originally designed to run on the 80286 chip, Windows eventually found itself working on the 80386 chip, albeit with modifications to make it run more efficiently. But it was not until 1991 before Windows was stable enough to have an impact on the industry.

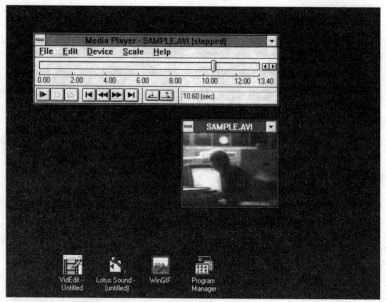

Figure 1.1 Multiple programs running under Windows

When Windows 3.0 arrived in 1991 the IBM PC industry took a step forward. Windows gave the PC a way of working with software, such as a spreadsheet, database or music program, using a mouse, icons and windows, which allowed more than one program to run and be visible on screen at the same time (see Figure 1.1).

But more dramatic was an ease of use that the PC had never had before. MS-DOS required the owner of a PC to remember a complex set of commands, and the syntax with which they are used, in order to perform even the most mundane task. Windows removed all of this and with its graphical nature provided a sophisticated and flexible operating system for multimedia software.

What of multimedia's real usefulness? From the small corner store to the large conglomerate there are myriad different recognised uses and benefits from multimedia. These include business presentations, training, information distribution, point-of-sale terminals, education/learning, photo albums, interactive books, reference books and so on. Let's look at a few.

The average manager or sales person will have to make a business presentation sometime during their career. Most people still use overhead foil projectors and paper handouts with such presentations, but in the 1990s we should really be making use of multimedia technology to solve this business task. Let's face it. Sitting through a presentation and watching someone flick through 30 slides is not fun. But multimedia can make all this information fun, and far more understandable to an audience.

Multimedia can also be used to make a presentation look more professional. Imagine that you are making a presentation to your managing director as part of a sales pitch to obtain more money for a project. Imagine using a colour overhead projector attached to a notebook computer that has been modified to support multimedia.

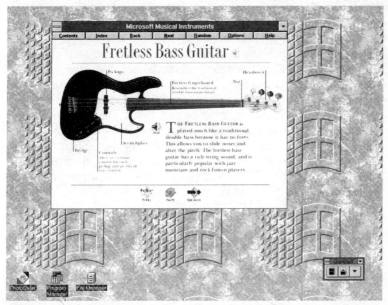

Figure 1.2 *Musical Instruments* from Microsoft combines text, stereo sound and images

So, for example, instead of using a slide to describe a new factory or office block, a mix of still images and digital video clips taken using a camcorder could be played with an overlaid voice describing the proposed building. These images could be mixed with diagrams and charts, and high quality audio (Figure 1.2) could be played to enhance the effect. All of this material could be used interactively: the presentation would not need to be linear and you, the presenter, could respond to questions by going back through sections of the presentation.

A managing director with a mind for quality should be impressed by such a presentation. The average business presentation, addressing a relatively small audience, is just the beginning for multimedia. What if we look at really big audiences. Electronic point-of-sale (EPOS) kiosks, those large cubicle objects that are springing up in many high street stores, are an ideal presentation device for multimedia. Trade shows, museums, banks and shops can all benefit from multimedia delivered using an EPOS kiosk. Showing a person what they are about to buy in graphic detail is the best way to convince them to buy.

If you make the kiosk interactive and invite a person to delve deeper into the information on offer then the selling capability soars. Imagine that a computer is on sale and your kiosk is trying to tempt customers. You could start with a picture of the computer and each major part, such as the monitor, keyboard, hard disk drive, memory and so on, could have a digital video clip, or animation, attached to explain its function. A voiceover can inform the prospective customer about the features. Images can be displayed around the screen to demonstrate how the computer and its software can be used. The kiosk can become an invaluable sales aid. Such a facility can also be used to demonstrate a wide variety of products: clothes, art work, televisions, hi-fi equipment, cameras and more. All are prime candidates to be sold via a multimedia sales kiosk.

Education is perhaps the one area that has already felt the influence of multimedia, particularly in the US. Music can be rediscovered by many people as demonstrated by Microsoft's *Multimedia Beethoven* application. This disk is an ideal teaching aid. Not only does it teach a person about Beethoven the man, but about the musician, his life and more importantly his music.

Another Microsoft package on compact disc-read only memory (CD-ROM) (see Chapter 9) is *Dinosaurs* (Figure 1.3). This is stacked with information on the long dead giants that roamed the Earth. Text, voiceovers from expert archaeologists and digital video clips are all used to draw a user into the disk and bring dinosaurs back to life.

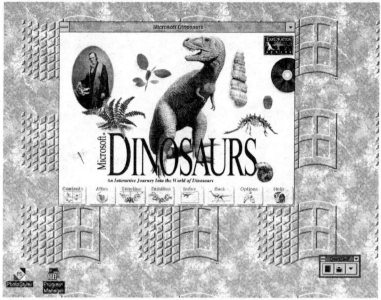

Figure 1.3 *Dinosaurs* is an educational program

These are just a few of the potential uses for multimedia. However, the boundaries of its use are unlimited and just about any subject can be covered by multimedia in a variety of delivery mechanisms. The features that can be provided by this technology are restricted only by how much money you can throw at a problem, or given a large bank balance, by your imagination.

One area that is sure to help the growth of this technology is entertainment. Games are enjoyed by young and old, with stereo sound and digital video clips being used to make games more and more realistic. However, the industry must be careful where it goes with its passion for 'reality'. Sega has already caused a furore with a CD-based games system after a game was developed that used movie quality images of scantily-clad women to enhance the game.

Philips CD-I system was one of the first interactive multimedia systems to have the *Joy of Sex* produced on it. The CD uses the CD-I full motion video (FMV) expansion box to use real video footage as an educational tool. The first soft-porn movie has also made its way onto CD as a digital film.

The entertainment industry has never been that efficient at monitoring just how far it takes technology, particularly when young minds can be affected, but government legislation has been introduced in order to make companies think before they act.

Entertainment products will range from such adult software to more innocent games, such as Virgin's *The 7th Guest* and *Dune*, a computer re-enactment of the classic David Lynch science fiction movie.

In *Dune* digital speech and actual footage from the Lynch movie have been stored on a CD. The incredible storage capacity of the CD, some 600 megabytes plus, makes it an ideal medium on which to store multimedia software. But there is more about CD-ROMs in Chapter 9.

Multimedia is invading the consumer and computer worlds at high speed. In the US around $700m is spent every day on entertainment and computer companies want to get a cut of this huge pile of cash through technology like multimedia.

## —— What about the future? ——

Over the next few years multimedia can only get better. More and more powerful computers will be launched at a price that many of us can easily afford. One technology that is closely linked to multimedia and will undoubtedly make an impact is virtual reality (VR).

A lot has been said and written over the last 20 years about VR, with some making sense and a lot of it being complete gibberish. So let's define the technology before we go on to talk about it. In its simplest form VR is the creation of a virtual world with which we, the users, can interact. It could be anything from a computer generated simulation of an ancient Egyptian temple to a 3D representation of somebody's heart and vital organs. Either way, the important part of VR is the fact that we can become part of it and actually believe it is real.

Any serious reader of science fiction books will recognise the name of William Gibson, and even if you have never heard of him, his book *CyberPunk*, is a legend. Gibson paints the picture of computer users, or hackers, becoming so involved in their computers that they physically plug, or jack, themselves into computer hardware. Their brain cells and neural pathways become interlinked with the digital bits and bytes of a computer.

This is fine in the confines of a book, or a movie like *The Lawnmower Man*, but for mere mortals like ourselves the idea of plugging into a computer can seem pretty far fetched. There is research going on into making a computer understand how a brain works and to then interact with it. But the product of such technology is years away. So how do we achieve a VR world like Gibson's?

We don't!

But with today's technology we can travel a long way down the road of creating a VR world we can see, touch and even interact with. Even if it is only inside a computer's memory subsystem – and not plugged into our left ear. To achieve this we have to enter the world of teledildonics. This odd technology, with an even odder name, is based around the concept of taking human movements – hand, foot, leg and head – and mimicking them inside a computer in real time. By real time we mean that as soon as you move your hand left the hand inside the computer moves left. The faster a computer can achieve this, the more realistic the VR world will be.

One of the earliest devices ever created in the VR community was the DataGlove, a sort of exo-skeloton that records every movement of a hand, right down to bends in the knuckle, and transmits data relating to the movement back to a computer. A complex graphics package on the computer can then be used to draw a 3D replica of the hand and its movements.

NASA has worked extensively in this field as part of its space exploration projects. Think how safe it would be if a computer hand could be used to perform complex operations accurately outside a space ship, such as when the shuttle crew repaired the Hubble telescope.

The next function of the DataGlove is to put the computer hand movements to good use. At this point imagination comes into its own. Just about any use can be made of the DataGlove: surgery, aircraft flight training, car driving, music, painting, anything.

There has also been work done to create all-over DataGloves which can calculate any movement of the human body. But just think about the computer power needed to calculate the millions of individual movements the human body is capable of making. That's more than the average PC can accomplish, that's for certain. So we have to look a bit closer to home for the use of VR in the near future.

So far we have talked about the replication of movement by a computer system, and not disclosed how a user of VR will view these computer generated images. The average computer monitor is two-dimensional with some limited three-dimensional features, and therefore of no use to a 3D technology like VR.

What is needed is a new viewing technology that fools the human eye into thinking it is seeing images in 3D. Fortunately, human eyes are easily fooled and computer engineers have created what are called stereoscopic headsets. Without going into detail these headsets are based around colour liquid crystal displays (LCD), one mounted over each eye.

The images displayed on the two screens fool the brain into thinking it is seeing three dimensions. This is nice and simple, but the only problem is that the quality is pretty poor at the moment, and very expensive. Scientists and engineers are working furiously at mastering this technology, with Sega wanting to develop a home version for games, but unfortunately the really good headsets are expensive. And the inexpensive are generally pretty poor.

So we have a stereoscopic headset, DataGlove and even a Data BodyGlove. All mixed together we have a lot of expensive technology and nothing to do with it. So what about examples of business sectors where VR can be used?

The architectural world is a perfect example where VR could really make an impact. The average architect or computer aided design (CAD) engineer spends his/her life creating a line drawing of a new office, tower block or car. If they are lucky their company has invested in a drawing package that can shade a CAD drawing to make it look more lifelike. But what if a special VR package was used to take this two dimensional image and turn it into a 3D model that can be walked around/through and then interacted with? Imagine the potential business benefit of actually letting a would-be home owner walk around their as yet unbuilt home to see if it's what they want. You could even give them the option of moving a table or a chair around to see how it changes the layout of a room.

Education is another arena where VR can make an impression. The Guggenheim Museum in New York has developed, in conjunction with chip maker Intel and Thomas Dolby the musician, a VR system designed to allow a visitor to enter the world of a Virtual String Quartet.

The system uses a DataGlove, stereoscopic headset and high quality spacialised sound (spacialised sound is a system whereby sound appears to emanate from within a VR world. For example, a bang could sound like it came from behind you even though nothing is behind you) and a lot of high quality programming.

Thomas Dolby is a real believer in the idea that sound is the mechanism through which a person will really believe in a VR world. He may be right ... he may be wrong, but what is certain is that the Virtual String Quartet in the Guggenheim Museum is brilliant.

More and more institutions will follow the lead of the Guggenheim Museum. It may take several years but eventually many of the world's museums and art galleries will allow you to sample the delights of years gone by via interactive technology like multimedia and VR.

# 2
# OPERATING SYSTEMS FOR MULTIMEDIA

Without an operating system the average computer is just a useless piece of hardware, and expensive hardware at that. Operating system software brings a computer to life and over the last few years the leading suppliers of such software have attempted to build as much multimedia support as possible into their programs.

## ─────── MS-DOS ───────

When the PC was launched in 1981 it came with a simple piece of software called the Microsoft Disc Operating System (MS-DOS). The software was designed to add support for all the basic characteristics of a computer: keyboard, disk/data management, graphics screens, and the ability to run personal productivity software, like the Lotus 1-2-3 spreadsheet or Wordstar word processing package.

Little changed for many years, although Microsoft and IBM made some changes to their DOS software, often with dramatic incompatibility problems. DOS uses what is known as a character user interface (CUI) which means that all commands have to be entered via a keyboard. Text commands like FORMAT, COPY, DIR, RENAME are used to perform an action on a PC.

However, these commands require a syntax to be known in order to make them work. Every colon (:), comma (,) or slash(\) has to be in the right place in order for a function to be performed. For some people the syntax, or language, becomes second nature after a few years, and operations can be performed really quickly. But for the majority the DOS command line syntax is a nightmare.

# —— Apple Macintosh System 7 ——

In 1984 Apple Computer launched a computer that went a long way beyond DOS and gave us the core design from which multimedia computers would build. The Apple Macintosh computer has an operating system that uses icons to represent a program, and uses a mouse to guide a pointer around the computer screen, in order to perform a command that is hidden in a menu. Point at Erase Disk in the on-screen menu and a floppy disc is formatted. There is no syntax to remember: it is nice and simple.

The latest development of the Apple operating system is called System 7.1. Even now it is based around development work undertaken in the 1970s at the Xerox Parc (for Palo Alto Research Centre) into the human/computer interface. Although the work done by Parc engineers only really came to fruition when the Macintosh appeared, these far sighted computer scientists have been credited with starting the ball rolling on the multimedia road.

The Macintosh System 7.1 software has been designed to take advantage of more powerful microprocessor chips, namely the 68XXX chips produced by Motorola, and most importantly to handle sound and video clips. Apple has designed a multimedia language into System 7.1, called QuickTime, which allows it easily to manipulate rich data types. The Macintosh is a natural machine to develop multimedia software on, and its designers have put a lot of effort into making sure that every new development is catered for.

# —— Windows 3.0 and 3.1 ——

It has taken Microsoft seven years to take the DOS operating system and turn it into a flexible piece of software that can even match the Apple operating system. When Microsoft launched Windows 3.0 in 1991, the PC at last had a graphical user interface (GUI) that sits on top of DOS, and gives it a look and feel like that of the Macintosh.

Gone were the keyboard commands and in came a mouse, icons and pull down menus. Windows was subsequently upgraded to version 3.1 which was the first operating system to run on an IBM compatible PC that featured multimedia support.

With Windows 3.1 came a Control Panel which allowed software drivers for sound cards, video cards, animation players and any number of other third party devices to be configured to work with Windows 3.1. A number of basic multimedia applications were also included in the operating system. Windows was well on its way to becoming the standard operating system for millions of people around the world to use to run multimedia applications.

Bundled with Windows 3.1 and 3.11 is Sound Recorder, a basic utility that allows sound files to be captured and then played back, and Media Player, a program designed to play back a wide variety of rich data types without the need of the utility that created them.

For example, Windows 3.1 handles sound files that come with a .WAV extension (for WAVEFORM) and a number of software packages can create this type of file. Not every user of Windows 3.1 will have the same program that created the initial .WAV file so Media Player was introduced to make sure every owner of Windows 3.1 can play the files. Other Windows applications can be programmed to make use of multimedia data through Media Player.

Media Player can also play MIDI files, motion video clips, animations, sound tracks from a music compact disc (CD) and many other data types. In addition to the sound utilities, Windows 3.1 comes with the ability to assign sounds to Windows 3.1 functions. If you do something wrong then a beep, whistle or even a word, such as 'wrong', can be used to identify the mistake. This feature can become a nuisance and many users of Windows 3.1 eventually turn this off.

What Microsoft has achieved with Windows 3.1 is to take a fledgling multimedia industry and give it a foundation to build upon. A vast number of software companies could all work on their different software, and be guaranteed to have it work together. A sound program from company A will work with a video editing utility from company B because they both use the Windows 3.1 Control Panel (Figure 2.1). Such a foundation has caused an amalgamation of the multimedia industry which has led to the adoption of Windows by a large number of users around the world. Windows 3.1 is just what the multimedia industry needed, and in turn hardware and software suppliers have reacted with a myriad of multimedia products.

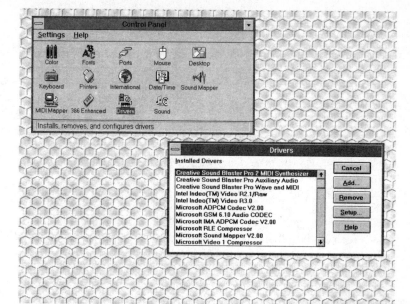

**Figure 2.1 The Windows control panel**

The next version of Windows will be Windows 4.0, or Chicago as it is code named. Chicago will be a very powerful piece of software that will offer a very powerful development environment for multimedia applications. It is also rumoured that the support for motion video images will be inherent to the architecture of Chicago. If this happens, the multimedia industry will have the first widely available, low cost video foundation.

# OS/2

IBM made a clean break from its partnership with Microsoft in 1991, although the two effectively split in 1987, after falling out over Windows 3.0. Whereas Microsoft felt the industry wanted a GUI interface that sat on top of DOS, IBM felt that a clean break from DOS was needed. What Microsoft and IBM effectively did was to make people choose between Windows 3.0/3.1 and IBM's own operating system OS/2 version 2.1. While Microsoft's offering retained a backward compatibility with DOS and the several thousand applications that work with it, IBM offered nothing to existing users. IBM expected its customers to forget DOS and embrace OS/2, even if it did not run their existing DOS applications.

The irony is that, as it stands OS/2 has always been a much better piece of software than Windows. OS/2 has a 32-bit design and is what is known as a pre-emptive, multi-tasking operating system. Windows is a 16-bit piece of software that simulates multi-tasking and is not pre-emptive. These differences make OS/2 a more robust program and more powerful when run on the correct computer. But OS/2's failing was its lack of backward compatibility and even now this still plagues the program. Version 2.1 of OS/2 has come a long way in its efforts to be compatible, and the software now has the ability to run both Windows and MS-DOS programs. Despite this OS/2 has failed to impress the computer industry, and over 40 million people have now flocked to run Windows on their computers, with only 5 million running OS/2. However with version 2.1 of OS/2, IBM has invested a lot of time and money building multimedia capability into its software. And you cannot buy a much better platform for multimedia development than a 32-bit multi-tasking program like OS/2 2.1. Unfortunately, the computer industry is full of dead products that are technically better than the products that killed them.

Multimedia places a lot of strain on an operating system and on many occasions often asks a piece of software to do two things at once. For example, an application may want a computer to play back simultaneously a mixture of audio, video or graphics and expect everything to be sequenced correctly and without any loss of quality. OS/2 2.1 is perfect for this process because it can multi-task, and demonstrates a particular strength when handling video images (see Chapter 4).

A comprehensive set of multimedia tools called Multimedia Presentation Manager/2 (MMPM) is built into OS/2. This toolset includes a digital audio player/recorder, media players that allow musical digital instrument interface (MIDI) files to be played, and a data conversion package that allows images and audio files to be converted. OS/2 2.1 also has a Media Control Interface (MCI) panel like Windows, which makes it easy for software developers to write their multimedia software to work with the 32-bit operating system. The MCI panel also allows for the correct media player to be loaded when a multimedia file is loaded.

MCI's appearance in OS/2 2.1 is a direct link of the close development work IBM and Microsoft once had. Both Windows and OS/2 2.1 use the MCI method of integrating device drivers for multimedia hardware and software into an operating system. As two of the industry's giants have decided to use MCI there is little to argue about here. MCI is obviously the way ahead.

The confusion between OS/2 and Windows, and to which is the best, will last for a number of years to come. Windows has become the *de facto* standard for multimedia software development and delivery, which is why this book concentrates more upon what Windows offers than any other operating system.

## —— The domination of Windows ——

In its barest state Windows offers little ability to generate multimedia presentations or software. A development tool, such as a programming language designed for multimedia, or an application like Microsoft PowerPoint 3.0, a business presentation package that works with rich data types, needs to be added to bring the whole thing together.

Microsoft argues that for multimedia to work it also needs to support the Apple Macintosh with its multimedia products. Although Windows 3.1 does not run on the Apple Macintosh, other than on the new Apple Power PC, there is a need for both operating systems to be capable of reading and writing compatible data types.

So where do we start? Windows 3.1 is clearly the established operating system for multimedia development and with the support of the multimedia Personal Computer (MPC) Council, an industry body whose role is to make Windows the standard for all multimedia development, it looks like Windows will continue to gain strength in the multimedia world (see Chapter 12).

Every major company in the software industry is looking to multimedia for future business, and their focus is on Windows. In 1993 the networking company Novell paid $17.5 million for a Massachusetts-based company called Fluent Inc., a developer of multimedia video products that allow full motion images and stereo sounds to be communicated across a network. Fluent's development work allows both Macintosh computers running the QuickTime video standard and Windows-based PCs running Microsoft's Video for Windows (see Chapter 7) to display networked images. It achieves this by running software, called FluentLinks, on Novell's Netware network operating system and it is this technology that Novell wanted to integrate more tightly into Netware. This in itself is very important to the multimedia industry because over 60% of the networked computers in the world are connected using Novell's Netware software. When video-conferencing and mutimedia software become more common Novell hopes its purchase of Fluent will stand it in good stead.

What is clear from all of this is that computers will need more and more power in order to handle this increased use of multimedia. The role of the computer operating system is also changing. Microsoft has developed a new version of Windows specifically designed to work on televisions, telephones, fax machines, photocopiers and other office equipment. Called Microsoft At Work this software is designed to prepare the consumer world for the explosion of multimedia applications as what we class as the television world impacts with that of the computer. This 'digital convergence' will change all of our lives and Windows again looks set to become central to the scenario.

In the USA, optical fibre networks and cable TV systems are being extended to deliver computer-based data into businesses and homes. All of this data is multimedia-based video, text, image and animations, and is therefore inherently connected to the revolution on the desktop. So before the data highway can become a success in the US, and then in the UK, the desktop computer world has to embrace multimedia.

In the UK British Telecom (BT) has developed a pilot project that allows home users to pay and watch movies via a system called Video on Demand (VoD). This technology works by having a massive computer, called a supercomputer, full of movies stored digitally, which can be connected to your home via the traditional telephone network. Movies can be ordered from the armchair without the need to go to the video shop. To make such a system available widely would require new optical fibre networks, which would cost around £14bn to install around the whole of the UK.

In the US Microsoft has joined with Tandy to develop VIS (for Video Information System). Basically VIS is a multimedia PC, running Windows 3.1, which has been rebuilt inside a box around the same size of a VCR. Take away a hard disc drive and add a CD-ROM drive and you have VIS, a fully functional multimedia entertainment box.

VIS has not taken off in a big way in the US, and in Europe it is unlikely to ever succeed because of the Philips Compact Disc-Interactive (CD-I) player which is making good progress in the home entertainment market. CD-I has gained the backing of Japanese and Korean electronics companies.

What VIS and CD-I demonstrate is the interest of giant computer companies like Microsoft, Sony and Philips bringing multimedia into the home. Although multimedia started in the business world it is the consumer world that will drive the enhancements in the future. Eventually the merger between the home and the office computer will be completed as digital communications takes off.

But back to multimedia. The hardware to make multimedia a success has long been available, but standards did not exist. It is operating systems that make standards come alive and the applications that run on them make the product a success. Windows 3.1 has set the standards. One of the greatest strengths of Windows 3.1 is Microsoft's move towards making its software object oriented (OO). Without going into too much detail on object orientation, this software design enables sections of software to be 'bolted' together, in much the same way as a child builds with Lego bricks, eventually to end up with a complete application.

Multimedia can be combined with object orientation because it is also made up of building blocks. Windows 3.1 uses Object Linking and Embedding (OLE) to bring elements of object orientation into its operating system. One of the first pieces of software to bring OLE version 2.0 into the mainstream is the Microsoft Sound System 2.0.

Through OLE a user of Windows 3.1 can 'embed' sound files or audio files into a word processing program or any other application that supports OLE. Modern software, such as Microsoft Word 6.0 can include multimedia files in this way. For example, mixed into the text, you might have a 30 second piece of speech recorded using Sound System 2.0, and a 10 second video sequence taken from a video camera. The process of importing these to the Word 6.0 document is simple and can be achieved with little or no skill in multimedia. Where the process becomes complicated is in the digital capture of both multimedia objects.

QuickTime is the add-on to the Apple Macintosh operating system that gives System 7.1 multimedia capability. To date Apple has shipped over a million copies of QuickTime since its introduction in January 1992 and over 500 applications have been launched that work with it. There is a Windows version of QuickTime and Apple has grand plans for QuickTime applications.

As time goes by the Windows operating system can only get better. As it moves towards being a true 32-bit operating system, with the release of Chicago, the software will provide a really powerful multi-media environment. Windows today is a sort of half-way house at which the computer industry has decided to stop for a rest; it is not that comfortable or functional but the best option we have at the moment.

Microsoft currently makes all the rules up as it goes along with Windows, which is a good thing and a bad thing. For multimedia the fact that one company appears to be setting all the standards means that multimedia can be adopted far more quickly. For the rest of the industry Microsoft and Windows is a bit of a bugbear. Many rival software and hardware suppliers believe that Microsoft should be made to relinquish control of Windows, handing it over to an industry organisation to co-develop. This argument will proba-bly be settled in the US courts, with Microsoft more than likely to win. In the meantime, multimedia is benefitting from Microsoft's growing domination!

# 3

## ── USING SOUND ──

### ── Turning up the volume ──

Multimedia is nothing without sound. The bang of an explosion, the sound of a baby crying, or an excerpt of Mozart can all be used to turn a series of images into something much more atmospheric. Before you make any move towards building or owning a multimedia computer a sound card should be considered first.

Early home computers like the Commodore 64 and the Atari 800XL, included microchips to produce digital sound. With the 800XL a chip called Pokey was used to supply four audio channels which could simulate a crude 'stereo' effect. But today's generation of games consoles from Nintendo and Sega produce high quality stereo sound as standard.

Unfortunately, the Intel-based IBM compatible PC was always designed to be a business tool and not a games computer. This is why a sound chip was never included in the original design specification, which is a problem when it comes to multimedia.

What was included in the design, and is still a feature today, is a keyboard speaker. This generates clicks when a key is depressed. The keyboard speaker can also be used to generate a variety of simple musical tunes and sometimes even crude speech can be obtained. But this depends upon the quality of the keyboard speaker and in all honesty the majority are dreadful.

Only in recent times have high fidelity (hi-fi) audio chips become a built-in feature on some Intel-based PCs, such as the Apricot Xen-LS II, which comes with audio capture/playback hardware as standard.

Compaq has worked with Microsoft to design a sound system called Business Audio. This system is built into the Deskpro XE family of computers. Compaq, like many other companies, has realised that without a standard for sound reproduction multimedia will probably fail to make a significant impression. This industry is all about standards. Any company that goes its own way will inevitably die. Just ask computer maker NeXT.

What NeXT managed to build in 1991 was the perfect multimedia computer. It had everything a person would want to handle images, stereo sound and motion video. Put together in a sleek black case the NeXT machine had one major flaw: the only standards it supported were its own. Eventually the NeXT computer died, leaving its operating system, called NeXTStep, which has moved on to work on the PC computer. The death of the NeXT machine was one of the saddest events in the computer industry. But it did give PC hardware and software companies a target to aim for: a brilliant design to aspire to.

PCs with sound built-in are few and far between. Fortunately, the Intel-based PC has expansion slots that can accommodate 'cards' which bring new hardware features to a computer.

In the US, where the Intel-based PC was first designed and sold by IBM, a market emerged for companies who built sound cards for the PC. One of the best known designers of sound cards is Adlib which effectively created the *de facto* market standard for audio reproduction on a PC. Even now any company writing multimedia software has to offer support for what Adlib originally created.

Games first generated a demand for sound cards. Initially, PC games were crude in their nature – simple bat and ball or maze games – which did not require good quality sound effects and the keyboard speaker worked well enough. Later, games increased in quality and stereo sound effects, sometimes even digital speech, became standard.

Take a look at the top 40 games on the market for the PC today and sound plays a major role in making the games more realistic and playable. An example is the game *Wing Commander II* (US Gold) which has an option for high quality speech which certainly gives the characters in the game a lifelike look and feel.

For this quality of speech a sound card has to be added to a computer and this is where Adlib and its rivals prospered. However, a lack of standards meant that each and every sound card maker ended up with a completely different way of playing sound.

The evolution of the Intel-based PC has led to a wide variety of sound cards appearing on the market. This lends a helping hand to the multimedia world in that sound can now be added to a computer for a relatively low price. The price is, however, driven by the quality of sound you want to capture/playback on a computer.

A company called Creative Labs sells a board called the Sound Blaster which can be bought from just about any computer store for well under £100. When added to a computer the Sound Blaster gives an entry point for multimedia by catering for digital stereo sound playback/capture and also comes with a musical instrument digital instrument (MIDI) interface, but more of MIDI later.

Most sound cards come with a host of software utilities that allow a compact disc player, amplifier or microphone to be used as a sound source. The software is designed specifically for use with the cards and gives a basic introduction to the features of a sound card. What this type of software fails to do is provide a way to create multimedia presentations or programs.

The first real development foundation for sound to be used as part of multimedia application came with Microsoft's launch of the Windows 3.1 operating system for Intel-based PCs. Inherent to the design of Windows 3.1 is the ability to use a sound board.

## —— Understanding sound cards ——

How do you choose a sound card? What you need from a sound card to make it useful and future-proof is a minimum of an 8-bit DAC (digital-to-analogue converter) that can sample at 11.025 kHz or 22.05 kHz, an 8-bit ADC (analogue-to-digital converter) capable of 11.025 kHz sampling, a microphone port, optional MIDI port, on-board mixing capabilities, the ability to synthesise four to nine instruments and an optional CD-ROM interface.

This is the base specification for a good quality sound board. If a board is purchased with a matching, or superior set of features, the sound part of a multimedia PC will be well catered for. But what does all this technical gobbledegook mean?

Before the different uses of a sound card are explained it is essential to understand how sound is made. A sound is commonly created when an object comes in contact with another. Human speech is created by the larynx which oscillates and interacts with air molecules. These air molecules move in waves and through the ears the human brain interprets these 'waveforms' as noises that over a period of time become known and identified. You can visualise waveforms as the same effect given when a rock is dropped in water.

A speaker attached to a hi-fi system works in much the same way. Magnets inside a speaker are used to oscillate 'cones' in relation to the music being played through an amplifier and this again creates waveforms that travel through the air to the human ear. This is the analogue sound that we hear every day of our lives.

The human ear can detect sound with frequencies between approximately 20 Hz and 15 kHz, although this top end falls as you get older. Higher pitched sounds have higher frequencies.

When a computer is used to collect a sequence of sound two distinct variables come into play: how much of the sound (be it speech or music) is recorded and, how often the sound is collected. This brings us into the world of digital sound. By digitising the analogue sound we take it from being a series of waveforms that the human ear understands to a series of numbers that can be understood and manipulated by a computer.

To digitise the analogue sound, an analogue-to-digital converter is needed. The sampling rate of such a converter is a measure of how many times a second it samples the sound that is being converted. Like sounds that we hear, this sampling rate is also measured in kilohertz (here, 1 kHz would be one thousand samples per second) and the higher the sampling rate, the higher the quality that can be achieved.

The recordings taken every second are known as samples, which in turn are made up of a number of 'bits' that relate to the sound waveform data stored in the computer in a sequence of numbers. Soundboards normally sell with a number of utilities that allow for a variety of samples to be made. It is almost impossible to state exactly how a sample will sound because the human ear differs from person to person and each and every sound card differs in quality. But here are a few rules of thumb!

The higher the sampling rate of a sound card the higher the audible frequency that it can manipulate. However, the highest audible frequency that can be achieved is half that of the sampling rate. The four most common sampling rates are 8 kHz, 11 kHz, 22 kHz and 44 kHz. This is where the trouble starts.

Digital sound has a number of points in its favour: the quality never degrades and it is easy to manipulate. But with quality comes an increase in storage requirements. Digital sound sequences can take up a lot of disk storage space – often megabytes of a disk can be consumed with only several minutes of audio to show for it.

The basic 8 kHz sampling rate takes up the least disk storage but generates a rattling sound that can resemble that of the inaudible British Rail announcer mumbling his way through a train timetable. The 8 kHz sample is low on quality but makes up for it with a minimum of disk space required to store the sounds. Sounds created using this sampling rate are not good for multimedia work but do come into their own for such things as voice messages embedded in a document.

Next comes the 11 kHz sampling rate which results in improved sound. The speaking voice over a telephone line is, provided there is no crackle, acceptable to the majority of British Telecom (BT) subscribers. This is what 11 kHz provides. It is an adequate standard for speech, although the lisping sound associated with sibilant 'S' sounds can be heard. Sound files are still relatively small using this sampling rate.

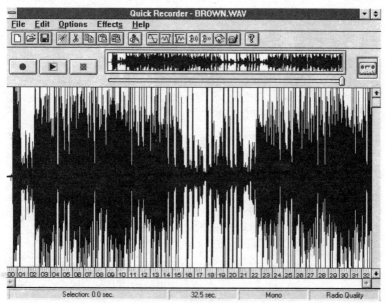

**Figure 2.2 How sound looks in the digital world**

The most common musical sound that many of us come into contact with is generated by a tape recorder. We have all had the irritation of the person sat next to us listening to a Walkman, and most homes have a tape recorder of some description. A 22 kHz digital recording sounds very similar to a tape player and is perfect for handling most sound effects a multimedia program will ever need. Speech is catered for, and so are normal sound effects – a dog barking or a car horn. What 22 kHz does lose out on is high frequencies such as bells or a high pitched scream. With this quality comes a high storage need which is a trade off that has to be thought about carefully. Do you have a large hard disk? If the answer is yes then 22 kHz could be just the beginning of a wonderful sound extravaganza.

If you are looking for perfection with digital sampling then you cannot get better than 44 kHz. Basically 44 kHz will capture a sound clip of compact disc (CD) quality. The storage space required is, of course, large. This type of sample comes into its own when quality is imperative. If you are making a presentation to the board of directors in an attempt to demonstrate the true merits of multimedia you do not use an 8 kHz sample of Mozart to kick things off. You forget storage problems and go the whole hog with 44 kHz.

After deciding which sampling rate you are going to use it is time to consider whether you are going to have an 8-bit or 16-bit sample. This choice will determine the amount of 'noise' that can be heard in the background of a sound file. Those in the music industry talk of 'floor noise' which is basically a soft hiss that can be heard between the sounds generated by a sound card.

The data captured during the sample process has gaps in it. Quite simply, the more data bits that can be captured during the digitising process the less hiss there is and the better the sound, because the gaps are plugged up. The hissing is reduced in jumps of 6 decibels (6 dB) at a time. This means that an 8-bit card reduces the soft hiss generated by a sound card by 48 dB which gives a BR train announcer's level of hiss. A 16-bit card reduces the soft hiss by 96 dB which is barely audible and gives a CD quality.

So now we know about 8/16-bit sampling rates, the thousands of bits sampled every second (kHz) and the problems with data storage.

# Software for sound cards

When Windows 3.1 came on the scene in March 1991 the whole software industry changed. A standard arrived and with it came a way to include sound in software that formerly had none. Windows 3.1 comes with a Control Panel and inside this is a menu called Drivers which is where all the special software drivers that control multimedia are configured and hidden away. It is here that sound card drivers are located. An up to date sound card needs to support Windows and normally comes with a set of disks containing both drivers and sound recording utilities for Windows 3.1. At the very least a utility included in Windows called Sound Recorder (see Figure 2.3) can be used to capture and playback digitised sound files.

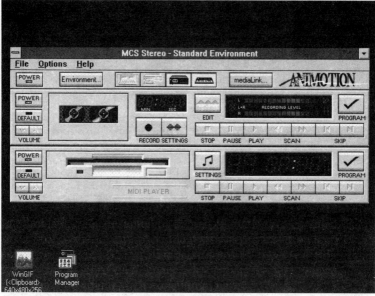

**Figure 2.3 MCS Stereo mimics a hi-fi system**

Sound Recorder can be activated by double-clicking on its icon in the Accessories windows (see Figure 2.4). The basic layout of Sound Recorder looks and works in much the same way as a cassette recorder, with play, record, rewind, fast forward and pause buttons. In the centre of the program window is a rectangle that displays a graphical view of the soundwave being played. Sound

Recorder can only capture a sound file with a maximum length of 60 seconds.

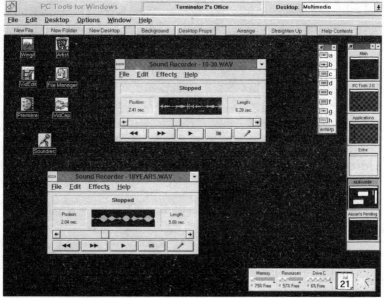

**Figure 2.4  The Microsoft Sound Recorder**

However, despite its limitations Sound Recorder does have its uses and is, after all, free. The 60 second limitation is a handicap for capturing audio sequences, such as your favourite rendition of Ravel's Bolero, and is of limited use for full-blown voice annotation. But it is ideal for short bursts of speech, sound effects and audio clips.

The Microsoft Windows Sound System has a 16-bit card that surpasses the buyer's guide feature set detailed earlier. Microsoft has designed and built a sound card that is as good as anything else on the market, but in the same breath no better than the rest. What makes Microsoft's offering better than the rest is software utilities. From the installation and configuration of the card to capturing an audio file the Microsoft software is clinically clean.

Version 1.0 of the Windows Sound System was pretty basic in its software offerings even though it did introduce the Voice Pilot, a way of controlling Windows and several of its business applications using spoken commands. In version 2.0 Microsoft has managed to clean up its software and now it supports not only Microsoft's hardware but a variety of other sound cards. By doing this Microsoft has made a second attempt at standardising the software needed to control sound cards. Machines using older sound cards, such as Creative Lab's Sound Blaster Pro or Media Vision's Pro Audio Spectrum card, are also supported by Microsoft drivers and at a later date the number of drivers supplied for different cards will expand.

Microsoft has built technology into Windows 3.1 called Object Linking and Embedding (OLE). Through the use of OLE Microsoft has made it possible for standard applications, such as Lotus 1-2-3 or Microsoft PowerPoint, to become multimedia aware. A sound can be captured using Sound Recorder, or some other utility, and then saved as an OLE object.

This object is then 'embedded' directly into another applications document, such as a spreadsheet cell or presentation graphics screen, for use later. Simply by double-clicking on the icon that represents the object it is activated with all of its features intact. For example, a 15 second clip of Bolero plays and then silences itself to become a quiet icon. It is simple when you know how. OLE can also be used to embed a video clip into a document, and is discussed in Chapters 2 and 5.

# ———— Buying a sound card ————

Sound cards have a common denominator: to make a noise. But each card manufacturer tries to differentiate its product from that of rival companies. We will now look at a number of popular cards to see how they differ from one another.

## *Genoa AudioGraphix 8600VLA*

Genoa is probably best known as a graphics card manufacturer and has experienced great success in this part of the industry. The AudioGraphix 8600VLA is a single expansion card that combines a high resolution graphics card with a multimedia sound capture/editing system. The two features combined on one graphics card do offer a benefit, since only a single expansion slot is used in your PC and in the multimedia world it is easy to use up all your expansion slots.

The card's sound capability is fairly good and comes with several useful utilities. Unfortunately, the sound electronics on the 8600VLA can only sample between 4 and 22 kHz which, as we stated earlier, is only capable of capturing cassette quality sound. The card is 8/16-bit compatible which does mean that hiss can be kept at a low level.

A 4 watt power amplifier gives the card a powerful output. Two missing features that limit the capability of the 8600VLA card are a CD-ROM interface and a MIDI interface. The lack of a MIDI port on the card also takes away an interface for a joystick which can make it difficult to play some games.

Bundled with the card are a number of sound utilities including audio recorder, stopwatch, timer and talking clock/calculator. The card comes with a Windows 3.1 driver which allows it to work with the device driver Control Panel and MCI interface. The software utilities can save data using compression software.

Additional hardware support on the card makes it compatible with the Microsoft Windows Sound System, old Adlib cards and Sound Blaster cards. This support makes the 8600VLA an excellent choice as a sound system for a PC being turned into a multimedia computer. The graphics circuitry on the card allow for a high resolution picture of 1280 pixels by 1024 pixels with 256 colours on-screen at the same time. This sort of graphics performance is another bonus when it comes to multimedia functionality.

Windows has a major problem when it comes to performance. The software often has problems displaying an image fast enough and a slow graphics card can handicap a PC. The 8600VLA does not suffer from this. Based around a 32-bit VESA Local Bus design the Genoa card is swift when it comes to running Windows. All in all, it is a good choice for a sound/graphics card.

## Genoa AudioBahn 16 Pro Model 3600

Those who want to buy a separate sound card to a graphics card may find the Genoa AudioBahn 16 Pro Model 3600 a better choice. This is an 8/16-bit card that can sample at 11.025, 22.05 and 44.1 kHz. The board uses a high quality Sierra Semiconductor Aria chip set which is capable of playing 32 simultaneous stereo voices at any given time.

Much of the performance of the Model 3600 is achieved with the use of a high speed digital signal processor (DSP) which makes this card capable of digitising and recording very high quality audio. The DSP also allows for compression technology to be used on sound files created using the card. A DSP chip is basically a processor chip that has been optimised to perform real-time mathematical calculations on numerical data which makes it ideal for handling digital audio capture and conversion.

Genoa appears to like doubling up the features included on its expansion cards. On the 16 Pro card the company has drawn upon the small computer system interface (SCSI) expertise of Adaptec. A SCSI interface allows for a high capacity disc drive and CD-ROM drive to be attached to the card. Both of these are ideal additions to a multimedia PC and as this book goes on you will realise the benefits.

The Genoa card operates in one of two modes: Sound Blaster or Aria. The first mode allows for the emulation of a Creative Labs Sound Blaster card which allows synthesised music, digital audio recording and audio playback to be achieved. Third party software designed to work with the Sound Blaster is also supported. But Sound Blaster MIDI, composite speech mode (CSM) and hardware compression of digital audio functions are not supported in this mode. If you want the full power of the Model 3600 card you have to run it in its native Aria mode.

All in all the Model 3600 is an excellent audio card. Its MIDI interface is a useful attachment and the Adaptec SCSI interface makes the addition of a multimedia CD-ROM player possible. However, if you are planning to buy this card and to then add a CD-ROM player it is recommended that you obtain a list of CD-ROM drives supported by the Genoa card. Not all CD-ROM drives will attach to the Model 3600.

The software included in the Model 3600 bundle is quite comprehensive. A package called Aria Listener uses the capability of the card's DSP chip to make it 'speech ready'. The addition of a microphone allows the card to recognise the spoken word. Once the card is installed a person can tutor the card to their voice and assign tasks to words. This is achieved by building a vocabulary of words and associated actions. With this capability a user can not only include audio in their multimedia application but make it possible to control a PC via voice.

Wave Lite is a sound recorder/playback utility that ships with the Model 3600 card. Although designed to work with the Genoa card this utility will work with any Windows 3.1 or MPC compatible sound card. This is a nice option and after testing I found the utility worked perfectly with my 16-bit Sound Blaster Pro sound card. This utility is easy to use and fairly flexible. Decide whether you want 8- or 16-bit sound, 11.05 or 22.05 kHz audio and away you go.

## *Media Vision Pro Audio Spectrum 16*

Media Vision is a well known company in the multimedia fraternity and one of its best products is the Pro Audio Spectrum 16 (PAS 16) stereo sound card. Like the Genoa Model 3600 the PAS 16 comes with a built-in SCSI interface and MIDI interface. This card is also an ideal choice as a PC's audio subsystem. One of its greatest strengths is the software that comes with it. This includes a simple to use recording package, mixer utility, and music CD player.

Monologue is a text to speech synthesiser which ships with the PAS 16 and allows textual documents to be read back with a simulated computer voice. Also included is a comprehensive MIDI control application called Recording Session. This is a flexible piece of MIDI software that will allow everyone from the novice to the expert to enjoy the wonders of making their own music on a PC.

# ———— What about MIDI? ————

The MIDI standard was first announced way back in 1983 as a method of connecting together electronic musical instruments from a variety of manufacturers, such as Roland, Yamaha, Oberheim and Korg. The result of this team effort has been to create a method by which computers can really start to make music. The acronym MIDI is an abbreviation of musical instrument digital interface. MIDI started as a way of enhancing the musical sound created by electronic keyboards.

In essence MIDI is a description. It is an electronic message designed to impart to a keyboard or computer a description of a musical event, such as when it started or stopped, and the state of the musical event, such as what frequency a note was, what kind of sound it was and how loud the note should be played. This information is sent as a serial stream of data which travels at a rate of exactly 32.25 kilobits per second. Each musical instrument is connected via a MIDI IN, MIDI OUT or MIDI THRU connector and is identified by a channel number. The cabling needed to link these MIDI ports is very basic: it is shielded twisted-pair cable terminated using a standard DIN plug.

For the most part MIDI is a technology that many users know little about. It's generally the case that sound software is used to play back a pre-recorded MIDI music file. Disks can be bought, both from professional software houses and shareware catalogue companies, that give you the ability to play quality sound, anything from Mozart to James Brown, without the trouble of knowing how to read music, let alone create it.

For those eager to sample the delights of creating their own musical scores a good starting point is to go shopping with Yamaha. This company has been designing musical instruments for many years and the addition of MIDI to its products has been a natural progression.

Windows 3.1 comes with a very simple MIDI Manager designed into its MCI Control Panel. This utility is designed to map numeric codes into musical instruments, and eventually sound. It works with whatever sound card Windows has been programmed to work with, such as a Sound Blaster Pro or a Microsoft Sound System, and allows MIDI music files to be played on a PC. Its availability is very useful, particularly when audio needs to be added to a presentation. By virtue of its design a MIDI file is smaller and easier to manage than a digitised wave file. Add to this a wide number of pre-designed MIDI tunes available to buy and suddenly you have instant music at your disposal.

Most shareware software houses offer easy access to MIDI files. Not all of us are endowed with the musical genius of Eric Clapton or Phil Collins and writing music is not easy. MIDI allows you to cheat a little. Let somebody else worry about the creative side of music while you worry about editing the MIDI music clip into the rest of your multimedia application.

# —— A smattering of MIDI software ——

There are not that many MIDI software packages on the market to choose from. If you do decide to orchestrate your own music the task of choosing a package is not a difficult one because your options are limited. But the software does vary wildly both in price and features, so shop around.

I recommend playing around with the software first before parting with any hard earned cash. Here are just a few of the packages currently available:

Twelve Tone Systems designed the Cakewalk Professional MIDI software which costs around £250 and offers all the basic MIDI functionality: recording and editing via piano roll, score or MIDI event. Despite its price tag Cakewalk Professional is a very good quality Windows MIDI sequencing package that lends itself well to use by the beginner.

Anybody linked to the MIDI software world will have heard of Steinberg's Cubase. The company has launched a Windows version of its software, called Cubase Score, which costs a steep £499, but offers everything the budding Beethoven would ever want. It is a wonderfully crafted piece of software, Cubase Score is a must for anybody serious about composing MIDI music on a Windows-based PC.

Other packages include Midisoft Studio, WinJammer, SeqWin, Rave, Musicator and SeqMax.

# ——————— MIDI hardware ———————

Earlier in this chapter we talked about how many sound cards have a MIDI interface built into them. This electronics is in reality, a synthesiser that can take a MIDI signal and turn it into a sound wave capable of being played by a sound card. Most sound cards use the same MIDI synthesiser computer chips, namely the Yamaha OPL3 chipset. This employs a frequency modulation (FM) technology to operate, and whilst this gives the sound card the ability to mimic the sounds made by a piano or trumpet, all the sounds generally sound synthetic. But a PC sound card fitted with a OPL3 chip set is probably the cheapest way to gain access to MIDI.

Sound cards are not the serious route into MIDI editing on a PC. If you want real quality you have to be willing to pay out several hundred, if not several thousand pounds, to buy a real synthesiser product, such as Yamaha's TG100. The TG100 is a small black unit which plugs into a PC's serial port giving the PC true MIDI connection and support.

MIDI is not a simple technology. The software and hardware can be a nightmare to buy, configure and use. Not all software works correctly with the hardware, with odd results being achieved between the MIDI software running on the computer, which thinks it is playing a harpsichord, and the £2000 Yamaha SY99 synthesiser which thinks it is being told to be an electronic piano. The whole world of MIDI sound technology is all about trial and error. So be patient.

Remember: sound is a critical component of multimedia. Without it we may as well pack our bags and forget multimedia's existence. The computer industry knows this and is making efforts to add sound as standard to many of today's PCs.

Microsoft is moving to make its Sound System 2.0 hardware and software a new standard for audio control under Windows. But companies such as Creative Labs, Westpoint Creative, Gravis, Roland and others will not roll over and play dead. While there is still competition prices should fall and soon every computer user will be listening to glorious stereo sounds emanating from their PC.

Before long most PCs around the world should ship with a sound producing chip pre-installed on their motherboard or a sound card installed in an expansion slot. So keep listening...

# 4

## —— VIDEO ON YOUR —— COMPUTER

—————————— **Video capture** ——————————

Anybody who has owned a home computer and has regularly bought the monthly magazines that are written for it will have read articles about digitising pictures. Plug in your video recorder or camera and with the press of a few buttons in a few seconds you have an image captured in your computer. It seems clever and easy to do.

The Atari ST, Commodore Amiga, Acorn BBC and a myriad of others have hardware available to perform such a task. The IBM compatible PC was long overlooked in this department, but now the marketplace is flooded with expansion boards that allow images to be digitised. And over the last few years a large number of boards have been developed that allow a PC to capture a contiguous stream of images as a motion video file. Video capture takes image grabbing a significant step forward. The problem with motion video capture is its complexity. The more realistic you want a video clip to look the faster the hardware needs to run, the more sophisticated the software needs to be and unfortunately, the more expensive the board will be.

In the early days of video reproduction on the PC, such boards cost several thousand pounds. One of the best known is Intel's Digital Video Interactive (DVI) board. DVI employed an expensive set of chips, headed by the i750 video capture chip, on an expansion board which cost over £2000.

DVI was capable of capturing high quality digital video but it had a major problem: cost. The actual production of video images that could be used by a DVI board employed a costly process of pre-production video compression that you paid for by the second. DVI made a modicum of impact on the industry before Intel eventually killed off the DVI board and replaced it with a much cheaper alternative – Indeo. There is more about Indeo later in the chapter.

Video images come from an array of sources: VHS/Beta video cassettes, camcorders, laserdiscs, television broadcasts and so on. Obtaining an image for a PC is not really the problem because sources are commonly available. There are estimates that over 100 million video cassette recorders are in use around the world. But the problem stems from choosing the correct hardware to capture the video image. And cost has a lot of say in that matter.

To understand video capture and its expense you first have to consider the dynamics of video images. In order to capture a single second of full colour motion video, from just about any source, you will have to deal with up to 27 Mbytes (MB) of data depending upon its quality. So what do you need for this digital revolution to take place? It has to be a computer based around a fast microprocessor with a big hard disk drive.

Let's assume that you want to capture a 10 second clip of your favourite movie, store it digitally and show it at 30 frames per second, and at full screen and maximum resolution. This would mean that up to 270 MB of data could need to be handled in that 10 second period. You can see why digital video needs a fast computer. The evolution of the Intel microprocessor from the 8-bit 8086/88 to the 64-bit Pentium chip means that we now have access, on the desktop, to a PC capable of manipulating real-time, full motion video images.

There is a wide number of video capture boards on the market: examples are the Intel SmartVideo Recorder, the Videologic Captivator card, Screen Machine from Magnifeye. However, the most popular video cards on the market allow for a video sequence to be played in a window and then a still image captured, or a sequence of still images to be captured.

Still images are important, but real motion video capture is the subject of this chapter. Video images are a natural way of conveying a message, but the problem with video stored in an analogue format on a video cassette or digitally on a laserdisc is that it is cumbersome, difficult to edit and even more difficult to distribute. So here we are with an analogue image that is ideal for conveying a message but a trauma to interact with.

The answer is to turn it into a digital video sequence that consists of zeros and ones, a language that all computers can understand. Once in this form the video image suddenly becomes as easy to manipulate and edit as a text document. Well that's the theory. And in its digital format the video image becomes easy to distribute to a wide number of people, even over a network where the video clip is transmitted electronically. And all of this can be achieved from a desktop PC.

The adage 'If you have enough money to throw at a problem it can be solved' is popular in the computer industry, but this is not the case with digital video because products will only succeed if the cost is low. Motion video capture boards have been available for a number of years and now the cost has been driven down to a point where many people can afford them. Chapter 7 will explore how software has matured in order to encourage the adoption of video on the desktop.

Just about every supplier of a video capture board has gone their own route with video capture and playback technologies and this has segmented the multimedia industry. Intel has its DVI technology, which then spawned the SmartVideo Recorder; Videologic has Digital Video Architecture-4000 (DVA-4000); and Screen Machine also has its own technology.

Slowly the hardware technologies from these suppliers are convering, and much of this is driven by Microsoft. Intel has developed a video technology called Indeo which is the backbone of its multimedia architecture. Indeo is a Compression/DECompression (CODEC) system which is used for the recording and compression of video data.

Here we used the important word in video capture – compression. It is impractical to expect natural video images to be taken and stored on a computer in their natural state. Even large desktop computers do not have hard disk drives big enough, or processors fast enough to cope with such a massive flow of data. This is an area reserved for parallel computers, such as the n-CUBE, which can be used to capture high quality uncompressed digital video images for distribution later.

Figure 4.1 shows how many capture boards, including Intel's original DVI add-on board, work. An analogue image, from a camera or video cassette, is fed into a video capture board and then stored in a digital format on a hard disk drive or high capacity optical disk drive. This is step one of the process. The video image stored will be massive and must then be sifted through via an off-line compression board.

**Figure 4.1 Vid Edit and VidCap being used with a Smart Video board to capture and edit a movie clip**

Step two is a long and complex process and requires a large hard disk to be used, and a costly compression system. Intel and IBM were amongst the first companies to offer an off-line compression service for owners of their digital video boards. This approach does not work for the vast majority of people and is frankly too expensive. It is also time consuming because the video clip is not ready immediately.

The correct approach is to compress the video data in real time. But this is not as simple to do as it is to write. Imagine that an uncompressed one minute video clip, using only an 1/8 of a screen (160 pixels $\times$ 120 pixels) is 50 MB in size. To make such a process work a real-time capture and compression engine must be able to take this 50 MB per minute data stream and slash it by 80%. The finished result must be flexible enough to store on the average PC.

Intel's Smart Video Recorder uses a one step capture and compression routine. Intel's Indeo technology can reduce a digital video file down to 9 MB in real-time, and is capable of displaying a quarter screen 320 pixel by 240 pixel video clip at a rate of 15 frames per second (FPS).

The frame rate of a video clip is critical to understanding its quality. Imagine an old Charlie Chaplin movie. To people who watched such a movie many years ago it would have been state of the art but to a person of the 1990s it is crude in its presentation. This is all to do with the frame rate. The highest quality frame rate necessary is 30 FPS which to the human eye looks totally smooth. The motion picture industry works on 24 FPS.

When a video image is being captured a frame rate of 10–15 FPS is suitable because the human eye is not very capable of telling the difference between these and faster frame rates. However, if the rate goes below 10 FPS the eye can tell the difference and the image looks jerky and Chaplinesque.

The frame rate is also critical to the size of the window within which a video clip is displayed. The bigger the window the slower the frames can be reproduced. It's all about pay-offs. A small window (160 pixels × 120 pixels) allows for a fast frame rate whereas a big full screen window (640 pixel × 480 pixels) makes for a dreadfully slow image rate. The best of both worlds is a quarter screen 320 pixel × 240 pixel image at around 15 frames.

Although a full screen image is difficult to display now, in the future this will not be the case. Intel has teamed up with a company called ATI Technologies to design and implement the Shared Frame Buffer Interconnect (SFBI) architecture for graphics cards and video capture boards. There is more about SFBI later.

What both companies hope to achieve is full screen, high quality motion video display on a standard 486-based PC. The early production samples of the new Intel/ATI SFBI board looks encouraging.

## —— The Intel SmartVideo Recorder ——

The Intel SmartVideo Recorder is what is known as a full length 16-bit ISA bus expansion card. Once installed in a PC it will reside in one of several hardware and software memory locations. Its installation is easy and managed via a software utility which comes with the hardware card. When the card is completely installed and the diagnostic software says it is working it is time to install the Video for Windows software utility. Three applications are added to the Windows environment: an upgraded Media Player, a program called VidCap and another called VidEdit.

Several hardware options need to be set before the board can be used. Three video resolution modes can be selected dependent upon the compression standard selected. These are 160 × 120 pixels, 320 × 240 pixels and 640 × 480 pixels.

The next major choice to make is whether to use the Intel Indeo data compression format, which compresses data as it is captured by the SmartVideo board, or the ISVYU9 capture format which does not capture data in a compressed form. The latter option, as you would imagine, requires a lot more disk space to store images. You can of course compress the data later as a separate step.

Two more compression settings then have to be set: key frames and the compressor gauge. A key frame is a video frame that holds all the video information that is being transmitted to the SmartVideo card. Any other frame that is not a key frame is called a 'difference' or 'delta' frame which only holds information about the pixels that are different from the preceding frame.

A key frame is set, by default at installation, as every third frame. The number of key frames captured in a recording affects two things: the size of the captured file and the quality of image. The settings of the key frame go from zero to three.

If you are capturing a sequence that has a lot of motion in it – such as a car chase or a flight of aircraft – you can set the number of key frames to one. This will increase the size of the capture file, but at the same time capture the most video information. Setting the key frame to one will also help give better playback quality if the captured file is to be shown on a lower performance machine to the one that captured it. For example, a really fast Pentium-based PC could be used to make the AVI file but a much slower 486SX-based PC could be used to play it back later.

The converse to this setting is when a video camera is being used to grab a close up of a person's face. This would then require a key frame setting of two or three.

Cameras are not the only way of sending information to an Intel SmartVideo board. The domestic VCR is a common device and just about every home has one. The VCR is an ideal source for video images because unlike a camera it allows you to have a number of attempts at capturing a video sequence. This will allow you to play around with capture settings to check which is best for the video sequence you want to capture.

But the standard video recorder does have a few problems. The image sent from a VCR through a composite video cable unfortunately has a pattern of distortion at the top which manifests itself as a sort of 'tear' at the top of the screen. This can ruin an otherwise perfect video sequence. This loss of signal is caused by a weak synchronisation signal from a VCR which the Intel board unfortunately picks up. This signal loss is most common in 'cheap' VCRs, so a good quality SVHS machine will fix this problem. Super-VHS VCRs are capable of outputting a video sequence of a much higher line resolution.

If you really want a perfect digital video capture a laserdisc player, such as a Philips Matchline, can be used. The images on a laserdisc are already stored digitally which means that a video card captures a truly perfect video and audio image.

However, the SmartVideo card can be used for more than just capturing sequences of images from a VCR or laserdisc player. A high quality capture of a single frame, which can then be saved as a bitmap (BMP) file, can be captured by the Intel board. The image can then be used as part of a business presentation, as discussed in Chapter 1, or as a Windows background (see Figure 4.2).

This action can be performed using the following sequence:

1. Start the VidCap program by double clicking on its Windows icon.

2. When the program is running you need to select Options and then Video Format from the menu selections.

3. Choose the ISVYU9 video format and the 640 × 480 pixel resolution and click the OK button.

4. Make sure that a video source is entering the board and then cue up a tape to where you want to capture from.

5. Choose the Capture button and select to capture Frames.

6. Every time you click on the capture button a single frame of the video sequence will be captured.

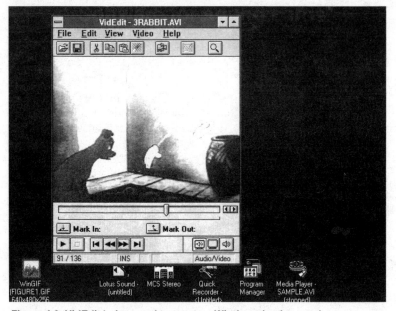

**Figure 4.2  VidEdit being used to create a Windows background**

7. Then you need to select File and choose the Save File option to save the captured image as a file.

8. This file can then be loaded into the VidEdit program which will allow a single frame to be edited in a paint program, or the Video for Windows BitEdit utility.

# ——— Other video capture boards ———

Intel is not the only company on the market offering good quality video capture boards compatible with Video for Windows. With a low price tag comes the Videologic Captivator board which is a 16-bit half length ISA card much like the SmartVideo board.

This board will accept two video signals – composite or S-Video – and works in either the NTSC or PAL television formats (NTSC is the US standard, while PAL is used in the UK). Captivator can capture images which range from 32 × 32 pixels to 640 × 480 pixels and supports 8-, 16- and 24-bit image colour palettes. The board also supports the Videologic YUV packed format which allows a file to be captured with a colour depth similar to a 16-bit image but only taking up a file size similar to an 8-bit image.

One of the real strengths of this card is its ability to support both NTSC and PAL television formats and to take video signals from the two sources. As with Intel's capture board the Captivator needs to have its own memory input/output (I/O) address and hardware interrupt setting. These can be automatically configured by installation software which makes fitting the card easy.

When you are capturing a video sequence it is best to play around with the different settings of a card in order to figure out its capabilities. Videologic recommends an initial setting of a small frame size (160 × 120 pixels) using the YUV format with a frame capture rate of 15 FPS.

The table here will allow you to calculate the final size of a captured video clip. It shows frame width, frame height, capture rate (FPS), duration (seconds) and finally the size of the capture file. The equation of

width $\times$ height $\times$ rate $\times$ duration = the file size in bytes

| Frame width (pixels) | | Frame height (pixels) | | Capture rate (FPS) | | Duration (seconds) | | File Size (MB) |
|---|---|---|---|---|---|---|---|---|
| 160 | $\times$ | 120 | $\times$ | 15 | $\times$ | 60 | = | 17.5 |

As you can see even a relatively small image makes for a pretty big file size. If you then move from 8-bit to 16-bit or 24-bit colour you need to multiply the file size by two (35 MB) or three (52.5 MB), respectively. But just think about the size of file when you leave most of these settings but increase the size of the image.

The Captivator board uses its own capture and edit software but can easily make use of the Video for Windows software as well.

If the Intel SmartVideo board or Videologic Captivator does not offer a high enough level of quality then Videologic also supplies a much more expensive capture board set called MediaSpace. This board will set you back a couple of thousand pounds so it is not a trivial toy to play with. But it is well worth the money when you see the quality results.

MediaSpace is made up of two full length boards. The first is based around proprietary video compression hardware called DVA-4000 with the second card called MediaSpace. The cards plug into each other and together they make up a very powerful digital video combination.

The Videologic software that controls the two cards is called the MIC System II, which offers great flexibility over the two cards. But the choice is yours and is basically driven by how much cash you have. If you have enough money then MediaSpace from Videologic is the best option, but a limited budget will be best spent on the Intel SmartVideo board.

Videologic teamed up with IBM in 1993 to develop low-cost silicon chips that add video capability to an average PC and a prototype of its work with IBM has been developed. This is the 928MOVIE video card which runs six times faster than a standard VGA card and can display up to 16.7 million colours at any one time at a resolution up to 1280 × 1024 pixels. The card has been optimised to play low resolution video images, such as those easy to capture 'postage stamp' 1/8th screen images at full screen resolution. Videologic claims it is just 'like having a VCR in your PC!' The graphics card also has a 16-bit stereo sound system which is compatible with the Microsoft Sound System, and supports both the Adlib and Sound Blaster sound formats. Videologic has worked extensively on a custom silicon chip, based around its DVA4000 video graphics processor, to power 928MOVIE. Prices for the card start at around £300 with no audio support and rise to about £400 with sound.

Much of the power of 928MOVIE is derived from its use of the VESA Media Channel Architecture (VMC). You could say that VMC is a direct competitor to Intel's SFBI. VMC is a way of giving a video card, such as the 928MOVIE, a simple and fast way of connecting into a PC's graphics subsystem. For VMC to work it needs to be added to a PC that has support for VMC on its motherboard, or via a 928MOVIE board.

Eventually Videologic and IBM want to see derivatives of 928MOVIE built directly onto a PC's motherboard and acting as an integral part of a PC. It could become as common a technology as a floppy disc drive.

# Breaking the law

Throughout this Chapter we have discussed the technology of capturing a video sequence. However, most video images on video cassettes and laser disks are copyright material.

Therefore, if you wish to use existing video material, you need to hunt around for as many royalty free video sequences as you can. There are several companies now producing CDs full of video clips which can be redistributed within your own applications. If you buy Video for Windows from Microsoft a CD is included with a whole host of video clips on it. Everything from aircraft to horses is included. Although the majority of the images are not very stimulating they do give a substantial media base to build from and do form the beginnings of your own multimedia data library.

You also have the option of using your own video camera and going out to make your own video clips.

The copyright law also applies to still images and audio files.

However, there are several uncertainties in the law surrounding the issue of re-touching images and video clips. What happens if you take a digital picture of Sylvester Stallone from a movie source, edit the colours and then cut off pieces of his torso and rearrange them? Can you then claim your own copyright for the newly created image, or is the copyright still in the possession of the original creator? My money is still on the illegal nature of digitising this sort of material. Take care. Five years ago a slight copyright indiscretion might have been overlooked but these days everything is taken more seriously by TV and film companies.

If you desperately want to use a sequence from Terminator 2 or South Pacific you could always contact the originator of the material and license it.

# Video in business

Microsoft's Video for Windows system is a method of playing video images on a PC without the need for expensive hardware. Intel's Indeo allows video images to be 'grabbed' (the term for transferring an analogue picture from a camera or video recorder into a computer's memory) and then stored in a format that Video for Windows can play back at a later date.

The whole issue of videoconferencing and desktop video playback is driven by the idea that business users can be offered richer sort of data. For example, a memo from the managing director of a company can tell an employee a lot of things but lacks any feeling or emotion. It is far easier to tell if an MD is angry or happy if you can see their face. Video could give this sort of empathy between staff.

The shop floor of a car manufacturer is another place where desktop video can aid in fault solving. Imagine that a worker has found a problem with a car's braking system but cannot visualise how to fix the problem. A half remembered training course of six months ago may be of no use. A desktop computer with an electronic car manual, complete with video sequences of how a braking system fits together, can refresh that employee's memory in a matter of minutes.

Intel and Microsoft see these sort of scenarios as becoming more and more common and want to establish a market. Video for Windows is steadily becoming the desktop standard for viewing video data clips on PCs and Microsoft has plans to build video support directly into its Windows operating system family.

Reading-based Iterated Systems has also targeted the desktop video market with a product called VideoBox. In 1993 the company released software that bolts onto Video for Windows and adds the ability to use fractal mathematical formulae to store video images on a computer.

Fractal mathematics was designed by Benoit Mandelbrot who used fractal geometry to create complex images by repeating the same routines again and again. Iterated Systems has reversed this process and plans to store video images in a small amount of space by breaking them down into their constituent parts.

One of the problems with storing desktop video on a computer is that it takes large amounts of processing power to play the video back using software only, and takes up massive amounts of disk storage space. Video for Windows needs around 10 MB of data storage space to store a one minute video clip. So if the MD's video memo lasts five minutes a hard disk with 60 MB free space would be needed to run it.

Iterated Systems claims fractal compression is the answer to this saying that its video CODEC add-on for Video for Windows will reduce a one-minute video clip as little as 1.5 MB. However, it is worth remembering that fractal mathematics requires a fair amount of processing power to work, so a powerful PC will be needed to use it.

Several years ago the thought of everybody within a company having access to a videoconferencing link from their own desktop would have been classified as too expensive, technically too difficult or crazy. Now this is not the case. Desktop computers have grown in power over the last three to four years to the point where this vision is now within the grasp of a large number of organisations. But videoconferencing goes beyond linking together six people located at different subsidiaries around the world via a camera, fast digital network and a desktop computer.

The telecommunications company Mercury has put a lot of effort into making videoconferencing a boom market and currently offers a number of different services to its customers. First any company interested in using a videoconferencing link but which feels the capital expenditure is too much can use one of several 'meeting' rooms in London. Each of these is fully equipped with videoconferencing equipment. Of course the office you want to talk to has to have a connection compatible with Mercury's. The company believes the cost of videoconferencing equipment has fallen by 25–40% each year to the point where it costs £10–20 000 to fit out a desktop videoconferencing computer compared with £50–100 000 not so many years ago.

Mercury talks of users creating project teams of staff within a company that work on a common development project but are physically based in a number of locations around the country or world. The use and cost of videoconferencing can be justified simply by adding up the travel requirements of staff within a company.

Let's use the example of a company with an office in New York and an office in London, both of which have ten staff. Mercury claims that a single videoconferencing system in each office, costing roughly £35 000 each, would comfortably meet their requirements. Added to this is a £130 per hour charge for the use of an Integrated Services Digital Network (ISDN) phone line for communications.

The capital cost of £70 000 is a lot, but when the costs of six employees flying between the offices three or four times a year – say

£4000 each per trip – are added up then the initial capital cost of a videoconferencing system can soon be recouped. What is then left is the £130 an hour cost of using an ISDN transatlantic communications line. Having said this there are still many times when a face-to-face meeting can never be replaced by a video link.

Suddenly videoconferencing becomes a fascinating reality that can be justified on cost grounds. However, there are still several snags to videoconferencing. To start with transmitting a video signal from a desktop PC down an ISDN line and then redisplaying it on another PC makes for a rather jerky, poor quality image. Even when many videoconferencing users are linked between two rooms in the same building the video link leaves a lot to be desired.

IBM and British Telecom (BT) have worked together on a PC-based videoconferencing project code named Coco, and the PC Videophone kit costs between £3000–3500. BT claims that 90% of UK business users now have access to an ISDN service via over 4000 modern telephone exchanges.

Unfortunately, it is still rare these days to see a PC-based video-conferencing system in use that produces an image in synchronisation with the voice. If a person suddenly makes a fast movement then the video system takes several frames to catch up with what has happened. The video can look like a badly dubbed martial arts movie.

However, when Microsoft's Video for Windows is applied to a network and used to extend the electronic mail (e-mail) metaphor the jerky images disappear – provided that the hardware used on the network is powerful enough. The problems stem from sequencing two video sources in real time, which takes a lot of processor power and the ability to transfer data around a network quickly enough.

However, e-mail does not need to be real time. Again we can use the example of a car maker and two design engineers working on a problem. Although both are working in offices separated by several thousand miles, video e-mail is a intuitive way of keeping them in contact. One engineer needs to demonstrate quickly to his associate how a problem with a car's steering wheel has been fixed.

A video camera could be used to shoot a demonstration of how to 'fix' the steering wheel. This image could be captured using Intel's Smart Video capture board and mailed across the world in a matter of hours to any engineer who needs to be updated on the steering wheel problem. The same sort of scenario is applicable to various businesses, such as travel agents, doctors, teachers, the police and so on.

The only problem with sending this sort of video mail around a network is its size. An average textual e-mail message takes up a few kilobytes of data not many megabytes as video does. Iterated Systems' fractal compression could be an answer to this problem. It is a problem that needs to be overcome before video e-mail takes off.

The early adopters of desktop video are more likely to come from the entertainment and leisure end of the spectrum than from the more traditional computers users. The games software industry will probably fuel the commercial development of desktop video as it attempts to market interactive video games that use actual video footage to 'bring a game to life.'

However, much will hinge on the correct storage medium for desktop video. The computer version of the music compact disc, called CD-ROM, is an ideal way of storing large quantities of data and is also cheap to manufacture, despite the money music companies charge for CD-based albums.

The desktop video industry is just waiting to explode. All the technical components are in place. It is now a case of waiting for a problem to come along that needs desktop video as a solution so that multimedia can be stretched to its technical limits.

# 5

# THE IBM COMPATIBLE PC

## —— The development of the PC ——

The best way to understand multimedia is to understand the computer that it is running on. The most popular computer in the world is the IBM compatible PC which is based around microprocessors and a variety of electronics, and is now used by some 100 million people around the world. But exactly what is such a PC?.

The birth of this computer came many years ago when the US semiconductor maker Intel developed a microprocessor (a chip which is the brain at the centre of a computer) called the 8086/88 chip. This has an 8-bit design which means that it works by processing eight pieces of data at any given time. Next came the 80286 chip which processes 16 'bits' of data at a time. The 80286 chip was eventually killed off by Intel and replaced in 1986 with the 32-bit 80386 chip. The evolution of the Intel chip design has delivered an amazing amount of processing power to the average computer owner. It is this continued development over the years that has led to the availability of a personal computer that can make multimedia a reality. Since IBM compatible PCs are designed around Intel chips, they can equally be called Intel compatible PCs.

The latest Intel chip for PCs is the Pentium, which has the ability to process 64 bits of data at a time. But the number of bits that a chip processes at any given time is only the first part of how its performance is measured.

The clock speed of the computer is also important. This speed measured in millions of hertz (MHz), has increased from chip to chip. The 8086/88 started at 8 MHz and the Pentium chip runs at up to 100 MHz. Intel is already working on chips that run at 150 MHz. Another company Digital has designed a chip called Alpha that runs in excess of 200 MHz which means that a machine based around it is very fast, although this chip is not designed for use in IBM compatible PCs.

Its speed and 64-bit design give the Pentium massive processing power that makes a computer based around it ideal for multimedia. With this power comes cost and you can expect to pay £2000 plus for a good quality Pentium desktop computer.

The processor is the essential component of a computer but there is still a lot of important electronics that live around it and make a computer work. To understand an Intel compatible PC you must understand something about its architecture, so in sequence we will look at video, storage devices, memory, expansion ports and the devices you can add to a computer to improve multimedia performance.

## —— Picture this: video adaptors ——

Without a video adaptor a computer is nothing. After all, if you cannot see a picture there is not much point moving into the world of multimedia. When the PC was first introduced it came with a poor quality black and white display which had a limited screen resolution.

With the introduction of colour displays, the PC started its long journey towards becoming a graphics workstation. The first such display was the colour graphics adaptor (CGA) which had the ability to display a limited number of colours and ran at a pretty low graphics resolution. It was a decent display adaptor for adding a touch of colour to a business application or for a basic type of game, such as Space Invaders, but it was in no way capable of rendering a photo on screen.

The CGA display was followed by the enhanced graphics adaptor (EGA) display, but it was not until the video graphics adaptor (VGA) arrived that photographic quality images could be displayed on a PC. This brought about major improvements in games. What VGA introduced was the ability to build an image that is 640 × 480 pixels in size, shown in 256 colours.

Within months of its launch the VGA adaptor was improved upon by an increase in its pixel resolution. Called Super VGA or Enhanced VGA this adaptor maintained the ability to show 256 colours, but at 800 × 600 pixels or 1024 × 768 pixels. Although the number of colours displayed is essential, mainly in order to make images more 'realistic', the screen resolution is equally important in that the higher the screen resolution the more images can be displayed (see Figures 5.1 and 5.2).

These pictures show a standard 640 × 480 VGA screen and a Super VGA 1024 × 768 screen. As you can see many more images can be displayed on the Super VGA screen, which is essential to multimedia. But now the problem. The higher the resolution the more the strain that is placed on the performance of the adaptor. This is linked to the fact that each pixel on a screen has three 'bits' of information attached to it, all of which have to be redrawn at high speed.

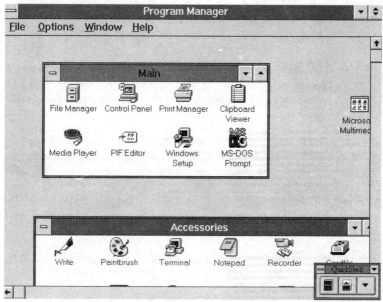

**Figure 5.1  Windows running in a standard 640 × 480 VGA screen**

With VGA, a PC has to deal with 640 × 480 × 3 bits (that's 921 600 bits) every time a picture changes, and with Super VGA this equates to 1024 × 768 × 3 (2 359 296) bits potentially changing 50 times a second. The number 3 in this equation relates to the assignment of a colour (red, green and blue) to each pixel. As you can see this is a complex operation that a PC has to perform just to create the image that we all take for granted.

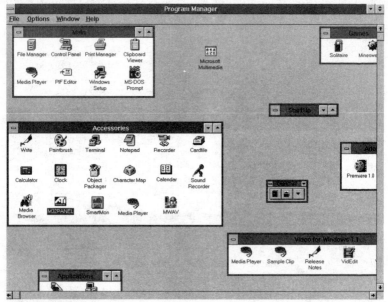

Figure 5.2 The much higher resolution of a 1024 × 768 SVGA gives a more detailed display

At this point it is worth thinking about the quality of the image you want to display. This means that 256 colours may not be enough to create real photo-realistic images on a computer screen. So after 256 colours come what is known as a 32K (as in 32 000) colour display and true colour. Both of these allow a large number of colours to be shown on-screen chosen from a palette of either several thousand or several million shades.

Both of these models allow for subtle variations in a colour to be displayed. To be honest the latter two colour modes are not needed for most multimedia applications, given that video sequences capture up to 256 colours and never worry about 32K or true colour modes. The majority of still images look pretty acceptable in 256 colours, and this mode is generally accepted as the standard for multimedia software distribution. Since the 256 colour mode is the most commonly used option, this software created in 256 colours can be used by hundreds or thousands of people and not just by the person who created it.

A multimedia software package that specifically needs a true colour video card would have a small target audience. If, however, the same program is written to work with only a 256-colour VGA adapter then the target audience suddenly expands to become millions of potential users.

For those looking to create, edit and then display the most realistic image possible then a true colour card is the ideal choice, but be prepared to cough up a good deal of cash.

After choosing the resolution a card can display, and the colours available you need to think about buying an accelerator-based graphics board for development work. The most common card in this product type is based around the S3 graphics chipset, which is designed to improve the way that Windows loads and then edits a graphics image. Other options include cards from Orchid, Genoa, Tseng Labs, the new breed of Trident cards, and Weitek Power 9000-based cards. Media Vision is a US maker of graphics cards that specialises in high performance products. One of its latest products is the Pro Graphics 1024 which can support a resolution of up to $1024 \times 768$ pixels in 16.7 million colours.

The hardware that makes up a graphics card is not the only important part. Software drivers that make it work with the operating system are essential to a card's performance. Almost all graphics cards will support Windows 3.1.

Although the OS/2 operating system is not as successful as Windows it does have a major advantage over Windows 3.1 that the part of the operating system that controls graphics, known as the engine, is written in 32-bit code, which allows it to run more quickly than Windows. The fact that OS/2 has a 32-bit graphics engine allows it to calculate and then display complex images very easily.

To end this part of the chapter I will talk about one of the fastest graphics cards on the market. The MGA Ultima is made by Matrox and it was the first 64-bit graphics card on the market. Although this card looks like just about any other VGA graphics card, when you see how it performs the differences become painfully obvious. A set of PowerDrivers has been developed by Matrox to allow its VGA card to work with Windows and to accelerate the performance of the operating system. The card will run from as low as $640 \times 480$ pixels to $1600 \times 1200$ pixels from a palette of up to 16.7 million colours.

A neat feature of the VGA card is its ability to mode switch on the 'fly'. Normally with Windows whenever you change resolution you have to install a new driver, exit Windows and then restart Windows in order for the new resolution to start working. There is none of this nonsense with the MGA Ultima card.

You can assign different resolutions to various keystrokes, such as pressing the Control and F6 key to move to 640 × 480 pixels in 16.7 million colours or Control and F8 to move to 800 × 600 pixels in 256 colours. The MGA Ultima card comes in a number of different configurations including EISA, ISA, VESA, MCA and PCI.

The ISA version of this card can quite easily outperform an EISA card, despite the claims that EISA is a much faster input/output bus architecture. There is more about ISA and EISA later in the chapter. This is an amazing graphics card that is ideal for multimedia use, but it costs around £500 with 1 MB of video memory (VRAM) or over £700 with 2 MB of VRAM.

The real performer is the 2 MB version which allows for more colours to be assigned as you move through the higher resolutions. So is this a good price to pay just to have fast graphics? If the card is being bought for a company, as part of a professional multimedia project then yes, but if the card is to be for personal use then think carefully. There are a lot of much cheaper graphics cards on the market that will do the job only a little slower.

Remember. Buying a graphics card is not an easy affair, so it is well worth reading a few computer magazines, especially those that do roundup reviews where they look at a large number of products in one go, and then use their findings to help you make your buying decision. You may also be able to test a card at a computer store ; there is no better way to make a decision than after having hands-on experience.

The performance of a graphics card is quite often measured in what are known as WinMarks. To give you an idea of the different performance levels graphics cards can deliver, despite appearing to be the same, several tests were performed on rival cards running in true colour mode. In this mode the Media Vision Pro Graphics running at 1024 × 768 pixels scored 30 million WinMarks. The Matrox Impression running at the same resolution scored 13 million WinMarks compared to 10 million WinMarks that the SuperMac Spectrum 24 scored at a slightly higher resolution of 1152 × 910 pixels. The Diamond Viper VLB scored 7.1 million WinMarks at a

800 × 600 resolution and finally the ATI Graphics Ultra Pro scored 3.5 million WinMarks at a 800 × 600 pixel resolution.

These figures are meant to give you a feeling of the different performance levels of graphics cards. Obviously, the price of these cards differs and it is always best to read in-depth reviews of graphics hardware before buying it.

# Storage capacity

In earlier chapters it was stated that multimedia requires a large amount of storage capacity. But how do you obtain this?

When a PC is bought it will normally come with both a floppy and a hard disk drive. The former is a drive that takes one of two types of floppy disk: either 3.5 inch or 5.25 inch in size. Both types of disk have been around for many years now and are the standard way of transporting data from one machine to another. The 3.5 inch disk is now the standard size, and the 5.25 inch disk is becoming rarer. But you never know, though when somebody may want to give you a picture or a sound file on a 5.25 inch floppy disk.

The main problem with floppy disks is their limited storage capacity. At best a high density, double density 3.5 inch floppy will hold 1.44 MB (or 2.88 MB on the newer drives, but these are few and far between) which is, to be honest, a drop in the ocean compared with what you will need for multimedia. A high density 5.25 inch disk will hold, at best, 1.2 MB.

These drives are read by a magnetic head which transfers data to and from a computer slowly. This is another reason why a disk is not a good storage medium for holding multimedia data. So where next?

A hard disk drive is a version of a magnetic disk that uses 'platters' to store data on. As with a floppy disk a hard disk uses a magnetic read/write head but it differs in that the platter is held in a vacuum which allows it to be spun around very quickly, which means that data can be written to and from a hard disk quickly.

By adding several platters a drive can then be made to hold large amounts of data. So a hard disk can hold anything from 40 MB to more than a gigabyte of data (1 gigabyte (GB) = 1000 MB). Three years ago when most people used a PC with DOS a 40 MB hard disk would have been a luxury. But with the arrival of Windows it soon became obvious that 100 MB plus is a good entry level storage point for a PC.

For multimedia use, a minimal set of applications would use up 50 MB of your hard disk. With average video clips needing around 10 MB each, and sound clips needing around 1 MB each, a 250 MB hard disk becomes a good minimum choice. Adobe Premier, which will be discussed in length later, can quite easily build video clips 20 or 30 MB in size, the result of which may be no longer than five minutes of action.

The speed of a disk drive is linked to the interface used to send data from the drive and into memory, where it can be processed. The most common interface on the market, which 99.9% of PCs come with is called IDE. This interface is fairly quick and allows two hard disks to be plugged into a computer at any one time.

There is work being undertaken by Western Digital, one of the leading makers of disk drives, to improve the IDE Interface. Called Enhanced IDE the new specification is aimed at allowing four disk drives to be added to a PC and will eventually allow a CD-ROM drive to be easily added to a PC, simply by plugging it into the back of a hard disk.

The next interface that is important to the PC and to multimedia is called the small computer system interface (SCSI). This is what is known as a parallel interface and is designed to transfer data at high speed into a computer's memory. Where SCSI improves over IDE is that up to eight devices, be it a hard disk drive, scanner, optical disk or CD-ROM drive, can be added to a computer using only one expansion card. The importance of this will become clearer later.

SCSI disk drives are not, however, cheap and as a consequence SCSI is more of a high end technology than a mainstream technology like IDE. But this is only of importance to the creation of multimedia software, and not its use by other people. Data created on a SCSI-based PC will run just as easily on a IDE-based system.

Hard disk storage is still pretty expensive. A 1.2 GB SCSI disk drive can easily set you back the best part of a £1000. As we have already stated this 1.2 GB can soon be eaten up by multimedia data files.

One solution is to use an optical disk drives, such as the Iomega Lasersafe Pro. Each of the removable cartridges in such a drive can store more than 1 GB of data. Hard disk drives, because of their fast access times, are essential to real-time, on-line editing of data, but not all data needs to be accessed all the time. The answer is to archive the data for use when you want it. Optical disk drives are the most common devices for this sort of purpose.

They are a hybrid of magnetic disk drive and the domestic compact disc (CD) player, in that a laser is used to etch the data into a cartridge. Unfortunately, the majority of optical drives are slow in their data transfer speed which makes on-line editing a problem. But they do make ideal archive units, albeit at a high price. Fortunately, a drive like the Lasersafe Pro is very fast, making it ideal for multimedia.

# Compression software

Another solution to the storage problem is to use data compression software on your hard disk drive. Over the last two years there has been an awful lot said about the problems associated with data compression software based around people who have lost data when this type of software crashes. This is, however, a cheap and cheerful way of making your hard disk store more data.

What the software does in effect is to look at each piece of data written to a hard disk and to find 'holes' in its structure. These are then removed and the subsequent piece of data written to the hard disk. The majority of data can be compressed in this way, although a lot of audio, image and video files already employ data compression of some kind.

The leading compression software is Stacker from a company called Stac Electronics, although Microsoft muscled into the data compression market in 1993 with a utility called DoubleSpace which ships with MS-DOS 6.0 and 6.2. Microsoft lost a legal battle with Stac Electronics and removed DoubleSpace from its software. But there are still millions of copies of DoubleSpace in use around the world, and you may have one of them. In version 6.22 of MS-DOS, DoubleSpace has been replaced by new disk compression technology called DriveSpace.

Microsoft has been criticised over the version of DoubleSpace supplied with version 6.0 of MS-DOS after claims from customers that they lost all the data on their hard disk drives. This is always a possibility when using compression software. Although this type of software does not go wrong very often, when it does it normally takes most of a hard disk's data with it.

However, as long as the working data held on a compressed hard disk drive is backed up, on say an optical drive or a backup tape drive, there is nothing wrong with using Stacker or DoubleSpace. To trust to a compressed drive that is not backed up elsewhere is suicidal.

There is also a performance problem associated with compression software. Because the data has been 'tampered' with to aid in its storage it has to be uncompressed before it can be used. This process sits in between the normal operations of the operating system and the application running on top and slows the whole process down.

The best way to use compression software is to have one drive compressed and one uncompressed. System boot files, such as DOS and Windows, should really live on the uncompressed drive, with data files located on the compressed drive. This means that in the event of a crash, due to the compression software, a PC will still be able to boot and the data could then be repaired. At the very least the system is still running.

# It's all in the memory

A computer needs memory to work. Imagine it as a blackboard that a processor uses to draw out its calculations. The bigger the blackboard the more calculations a processor can perform at any given time. Unfortunately, the PC brings with it baggage from the early 1980s when memory was limited and computers shipped with at most 640 KB of memory. This is chicken feed for today's average PC!

It is now common for PCs to sell with 4 MB of memory, or more depending upon their planned use. But no matter how much memory is inside a PC the first 640 KB is essential to the overall functionality of an Intel compatible PC. The first 640 KB is used by MS-DOS to run applications. It is known as conventional memory and everything greater than 640 KB is known as either expanded or extended memory, depending on the way a computer is configured. This is not the place to explain the differences between these types of memory, but Windows and therefore most multimedia applications use extended memory, whereas DOS programs, particularly games, use expanded memory.

Today's PC is like to have a minimum of 4 MB of memory but before starting down the multimedia track at least 8 MB of memory is needed. Four MB of memory is fine for playing back a video file or music file but when you start editing multimedia data it is inadquate. Software like Adobe Premiere will not run in anything less than 8 MB, with 32 MB recommended.

Memory and multimedia do not really go together very well. When a CD-ROM player is added it needs its own memory driver and a Microsoft file MSCDEX to operate. These files use up the base 640 KB of memory, and other device drivers, such as those for a sound card or SCSI disc drive, also eat into this memory.

It is easy for this 640 KB to vanish very quickly, which is where a utility program called a Memory Manager comes in very useful. In Microsoft DOS 6.0 and above, there is a file called MemMaker which is designed to look at a PC's memory and to find ways of hiding device drivers, such as MSCDEX, away in memory other than the base 640 KB. MemMaker can win back vital memory, but it has compatibility problems with certain games. Fortunately the software is easy to use and can be simply removed with a simple MEMMAKER /UNDO command at the C:\ prompt.

Other pieces of software that perform a similar function to MemMaker are 386MAX and Qualitas. These two software programs are more flexible than MemMaker but they do cost money, whereas MemMaker is free with the latest versions of MS-DOS.

Multimedia is a memory hungry technology and the simple premise is the more memory the merrier. A PC with 16 MB is ideal for running multimedia applications and when running Microsoft Video for Windows this amount of memory will ensure a fully synchronised capture sequence. A large amount of memory will also allow images to be manipulated more quickly.

# ——— Plugs, sockets and slots ———

One of the great strengths of the Intel compatible PC is that it can be expanded. Inside the PC are several expansion slots. These come in three sizes – 8-, 16- and 32-bit – depending upon the type of machine. Different expansion cards or boards can be inserted into these slots in order to improve the way that a PC works. Expansion boards can add network capability, more memory, improved video performance, sound, storage, and just about any other technical improvement you can think of. But before buying an expansion card you must know what type of slot your PC has.

The most common slot design in PCs uses the Industry Standard Architecture (ISA), or AT bus. This design has been around for many years and allows for 8- and 16-bit expansion cards to be added to a computer. The ISA slot unfortunately works too slowly for many modern processors.

Chips like the Intel 486 and 486DX2 are very fast and have a 32-bit architecture which is why an updated slot architecture called the Extended ISA (or EISA) slot was developed. EISA is a 32-bit design that allows data to be transferred more quickly between the expansion bus and a computer's memory, which in turn is attached to a PC's processor. Despite its improved performance the EISA slot is in limited use and expansion cards cost a lot more than ISA cards, which means that ISA remains the *de facto* standard on the desktop. People appear to put up with the limited performance of ISA because it is cheaper to fill expansion slots with cards designed for it instead of EISA.

The main reason for the lack of interest in EISA is cost. At the beginning of its lifetime, the 32-bit I/O (Input/Output) bus architectures demanded a premium price, mainly because manufacturers such as Apricot and Compaq based their high-speed network file servers around EISA. The only problem with the ISA bus is that it is restricted in terms of performance. With microprocessors running at 66 MHz, a 10 MHz bus architecture is just too slow. What was, and still is, needed is a new way of taking external data, be it from a networking card or a motion video card connected to a world-wide videoconferencing network, and feeding it to a microprocessor at a speed that does not slow the microprocessor down. The AT bus cannot keep up with the changes in microprocessor technology and the computer intensive demands that many users now have.

Some of the computer industry has moved towards a new slot design called 'local bus'. This is a high speed design which originated on PCs based around the 486 chip, bolting directly into the chip's memory bus, and was designed to accelerate graphics performance. The design is called VL and was put together by the Video Electronics Standards Association (VESA). To date a number of PC makers and expansion board makers have adopted the VESA design. Graphics boards based around the VL design, such as the AMI Power 9000 card, are pretty quick and offer millions of colours at high speed. The local bus design is probably the best choice for a multimedia computer. At the very least a PC's graphics will be accelerated, and many computer makers are including local bus graphics with their computers. (See Chapter 8 for details of how to build a multimedia computer.)

VESA VL is a 32-bit design and is generally implemented on the motherboard of a PC by extending the length of two or three ISA slots with additional pin-outs that allow data to be communicated between an expansion board, most commonly a graphics accelerator, and a microprocessor's memory bus. But even VESA VL has limitations. To start with, the architecture is tied to the 486 chip and there are many reported problems of 'incompatibility' difficulties with VL expansion boards. Many problems with VL boards are caused by the driver software that makes them work. Board makers have a tendency to write driver software that runs a board at its fastest speed and this is sometimes too fast. Video board makers can forget about the clarity of an image, or the quality of the colours displayed on-screen, just for the sake of having the fastest VL-based graphics board on the market.

However, VL has been a saving grace for many PC makers. At a time when it is almost impossible to tell one PC from the next – except by the badge and colour of the case – VL offers a marketing opportunity. Suddenly that boring old AT-based PC can be turned into a super-fast desktop machine.

The Taiwanese/Korean/Chinese motherboard manufacturing market has embraced VL in a big way. Look in any magazine for 'computer bits' suppliers and there is bound to be an advert selling VL-based motherboards for as little as £99 (without a microprocessor) but loaded with cache memory. See Chapter 8 on making your own PC.

The biggest problem with VESA is that it was not built on a solid electrical base but instead was 'bolted' onto what already existed. This gave VESA the advantage of being cheap and easy to use, but the price users pay is that it is not very robust and there have been some compatibility problems.

Intel has defined its own local bus architecture called Peripheral Component Interconnect (PCI). With its design Intel is hoping to harness the power of its high-end 486 and Pentium chips with a slot design capable of transferring data into a PC's memory very quickly. PCI has obtained some support but mainly at the high end. This is a better design than VL and it could well supersede the VL design.

Although PCI is technically superior to VESA VL you cannot forget that over a hundred PC makers are already making computers based around the VL local bus and almost none are using PCI because it is only recently available and more expensive.

When put side by side there is a 10–15% performance increase from VESA to PCI local bus, a performance difference that will benefit graphics, storage and networking. On the whole most expansion board makers are looking to develop both VESA VL and PCI designs.

## The colour monitor

The monitor is an important component of a multimedia system. Earlier in this Chapter we talked of a graphics card capable of displaying a resolution of 1024 × 768 pixels. Some cards will also display a massively high resolution of 1280 × 1024 pixels.

The problem with this sort of high resolution is that a standard 14 inch monitor, which ships with just about every PC, either will not show such a resolution, or displays a picture that is unreadable. For multimedia you need to use a 17 or 21 inch monitor that is capable of displaying a range of resolutions at a number of scan frequencies. Called a multiscan or multisynch monitor this type of screen is ideal for multimedia. The monitor on the front of this book is a Samsung SyncMaster 5C 17 inch screen – recently superseded by the Samsung 17GL – which generates a crisp image ideal for viewing high resolution images. It is not essential to have this size of monitor but after you have tinkered with multimedia for a few weeks you will see the benefits of keeping several applications running at the same time.

This means that an art package can load a picture, such as a car or a boat, and then a second application be used to grab a digital picture from a camera, and then a third application used to blend the two images together. The beauty of a big monitor is that all of these applications can be viewed at the same time.

However, if you are developing a multimedia program you must always remember that another person who uses the program may not have as high a resolution as you. So when finishing an application make sure that it will work at a 640 × 480 pixel resolution. The converse is true of an application being written on a 640 × 480 pixel display which is then viewed on a 1024 × 768 pixel screen. This is a difficult problem to overcome. Even the most professional software company can fall foul of this problem.

The multiscan monitor is invaluable because it will automatically switch its settings to suit a resolution. In general, just about any resolution can be achieved by a multisync monitor. A normal 14 inch monitor that ships with a PC will probably be able to display 640 × 480 pixels comfortably and may well extend to 1024 × 768 pixels, but this is not always guaranteed. When buying a monitor make sure it can work in the resolutions you want it to.

## The future

There is a new competitor to the PC now on the market, which has been developed by IBM, Apple and Motorola. Dubbed 'PowerPC' this architecture is intended to break computer makers away from having to use chips solely manufactured by Intel. The cornerstone of the PowerPC architecture is a silicon chip called the 601. Designed, manufactured and shipped within 12 months the 601 demonstrates how committed IBM, Motorola and Apple are to breaking the vice like grip Intel has on the desktop computer market.

Apple needs the PowerPC to be a success. The Macintosh computer, once the only machine to buy if you wanted a graphical user interface for your operating system, is losing ground to PCs running Microsoft Windows. Apple has to fight back in order to survive. Although its System 7.1 operating system is technically superior to Windows 3.1, it will not be easy for Apple to prove that its PowerPCs are a better buy than Intel based PCs.

For IBM the PowerPC desktop computer is a way to take its proprietary RS6000 workstation, which has done well in scientific institutions, and turn it into a mainstream open systems platform. The 601 chip is derived from several years development work by IBM and the RS6000 may now find a new lease of life.

IBM's priming of the marketplace shows an interest in making PowerPC a major success not only on the desktop but in a number of different third party devices.

IBM is planning to 'clone' the software inside a 486 chip that makes it work, called microcode, and transplant it inside the PowerPC chip. Called the PowerPC 615 this chip is claimed by IBM to run as fast as a 66 MHz Pentium chip and run all the thousands of Windows and DOS software applications. This also goes for multimedia software. Whether the 615 chip will be better than an Intel chip still remains to be seen. So far IBM and Apple have both launched PowerPC computers and their impact on the computer industry, and multimedia, has yet to be measured.

Motorola is a giant semiconductor maker with over 50 000 silicon devices in its product catalogue. For 10 years it has been in the shadow of Intel but now it has a chance to become the number one supplier of microprocessor chips to the business computer market. The company already has plans to help companies build everything from laptop PCs, incorporating a low-power version of the PowerPC chip, to super computers that use many PowerPC chips running in parallel.

The critical problem for PowerPC to overcome will be in convincing customers that the 601, and its successors the 603, 604 and 620, are faster and more price competitive than Intel 486 and Pentium chips.

The Pentium chip is make or break for Intel at the high end. It represents a legacy for Intel in that, while the x86 architecture dominates the PC industry, the Pentium has to offer compatibility with it. But by offering compatibility for the thousands of applications written for the DOS operating system Intel restricts itself from launching more powerful processors at a low price.

PowerPC had no users, it had no software community built around it, which meant that the designers of the chip could start from scratch in developing a processor that runs quickly but does not cost too much.

Another new powerful microprocessor that is not hindered by the success of the chips that went before it is the Digital Alpha processor. This silicon chip can run up to 200 MHz and offers a staggering level of performance. The Alpha chip is unlikely to have much impact on the desktop computer market in the immediate future.

The technical capability of a microprocessor chip, be it the 601, Pentium or Alpha chip is insignificant compared to the software that runs on it. The one common theme that unites every major chip architecture on the market is Microsoft's software, and more significantly its next generation 32-bit operating system called Windows NT. Even something as new as PowerPC needs Microsoft's support to succeed.

If IBM, Apple and Motorola do succeed in making PowerPC a success then multimedia will be one technology that is sure to benefit.

# 6

# — THE SOFT OPTION —

## ———— Development tools ————

In earlier Chapters of this book we have discussed the integral part that Microsoft plays on the multimedia industry. The company provides everything from the operating system that we all use on our PCs to supplying high quality CD-based software using every aspect of multimedia: video, audio, text and animation.

Microsoft also supplies a high performance multimedia software authoring tool. Called the Multimedia Viewer Publishing Toolkit version 2.0 this advanced piece of software has been used by Microsoft to put together many of its own packages, such as Cinemania, and is aimed at the publishing community. This is the area of multimedia that interests book publishers, be it Hodder Headline who publish this book, or any large business looking to publish any of their documentation. Multimedia brings publishing alive and Microsoft wants to take advantage of this.

Publishers need to use a development tool to design and write multimedia publications. However, one development tool will not meet the needs of every application being written. The software requirements for each category of multimedia – such as training, presentations, information kiosks, publishing, education, and enter-tainment – all differ greatly. For example, the tools needed to put together the *Oxford English Dictionary* will have to handle many megabytes of text information, text that must be accessed at high speed if it is to be of any real use as an educational tool.

Compare this with the software needs of an entertainment package, such as Microsoft *Dinosaurs*, which has both educational and fun requirements. For *Dinosaurs* to work properly a high level of quality graphics and interactivity is needed. In an entertainment, or 'edutainment' product a user has to be able to interact with the software or it is of no use.

It is also important to realise that with the different software tools needed to prepare an application so the skills of the author change accordingly. You have to know your limitations and work with people who complement your own skills.

Lets look at the electronic publishing needs of a large international company, which may have several thousand staff who regularly need to access style guides, reference manuals, telephone directories, help documents, training documents and so on. In a paper format this information is cumbersome, difficult to replace, upgrade and then re-distribute. One answer could lie with an electronic replacement that fits every manual and document on one CD-ROM that costs a mere 50 pence to make if enough are manufactured. But how do you put all of these words on a CD? How long will it take? How much will it cost? What happens when documents change half way through the writing of the CD?

These are all difficult questions to answer. If they are addressed then electronic publishing brings several key benefits:

- lower distribution costs;

- time savings due to easy text retrieval and improved accuracy of the business information presented to employees;

- improved customer service based on faster access to information;

- better retention of information;

- a possible strategic advantage over competitors.

So what type of software do you need to use to develop this sort of electronic documentation? Multimedia electronic books need little audio expertise, unless they are encyclopedias. The graphics expertise needed will vary from book to book, but what is most important is a system that can deal with a large amount of text in a sensible fashion. The development tool needed for this job must employ a fast word/sentence search engine and be equipped with fast and efficient hyperlink technology. Hyperlink is a method of indexing words that appear within a paragraph or chapter of a manual.

For example, in Microsoft's *Cinemania* software every actor, movie and award is hyperlinked with other chapters of the book. Generally speaking the text with the hyperlink is marked as a different colour (see Figure 6.1) and by simply clicking on it you will be taken to another chapter or paragraph that is linked to the first paragraph. If, for example, you search for the movie *Star Wars* you will be given a list of the actors who starred in it: Mark Hammill, Carrie Fisher, Alec Guinness, Peter Cushing and so on. If a biography of Alec Guinness is also on the CD, or a list of other movies he has starred in, then his name will appear in bold compared with the other text on the screen. Simply click on the name and a biography of Alec Guinness will appear. This is hypertext at its simplest. In medical books or encyclopedias hypertext links can be used professionally to help solve a task.

**Figure 6.1** *Cinemania* has information on thousands of movies. Here it is being used to look up details of *2001: A Space Odyssey*

It makes it easier to track down every possible symptom that causes a rare and fatal disease. A symptom could quite easily be missed by scanning page after page of printed text.

What is crucial to hypertext is an action list that remembers every link made between text held on a CD. Bearing in mind that a CD holds 600 MB plus of data (over 250 000 A4 pages of text), an action list of hyper-jumps becomes critically important.

# Multimedia Viewer 2.0

Microsoft's Multimedia Viewer 2.0 has a very efficient hypertext capability, making a superb development tool for electronic documentation. Viewer 2.0 uses a tool called Hypermedia to integrate its links into complex multimedia applications. The application has built-in support for text-rich software allows a user to navigate their way through non-linear bodies of text. Anybody developing with Viewer 2.0 can directly access pre-defined navigation tools, such as a contents topic finder, browse engine, a back button to retrace steps through software and a history feature that lists 40 topics (or hypertext links) most recently used.

The key strength of Microsoft's software is its ability to use hypertext technology to link text with graphics, audio and video. This is key to the high-end, professional finish needed for multimedia software. Instead of just jumping to a section of text associated with Alec Guinness, you can jump to an audio clip of him reciting Shakespeare or a video sequence from Star Wars showing him fighting Darth Vader.

The search engine associated with multimedia development software acts like a standard database application that has been customised to work with the peculiar way that data is stored on a CD-ROM. The search software will allow you to look for words, phrases, words in various combinations or specified proximities, and wildcard searches.

Many multimedia development environments lack this control over searches. Viewer 2.0 supports all these searches, plus the ability to search for a range of standard data types, customisable fields, multiple keyword indexes, topic groups, and multiple word-wheel options.

Database search engines are one of the critical technologies in multimedia CD applications. It is the search engine that gives a development environment the ability to search its way through hundreds of megabytes of text, graphics, audio clips and video clips in a matter of seconds. With Viewer 2.0, Microsoft has taken the hard work out of building a search engine because all the components have been put together. All you have to do is bolt them together, along with your data, to create a multimedia application. Viewer 2.0 is not the only piece of software on the market capable of generating multimedia software. Several others are discussed in this chapter. Viewer 2.0 is one of the best but it is not an easy tool to master.

How do you go about using the software?

First, you need to make sure that you have a machine capable of supporting the software. This means that you need the following:

- minimum processor: 80386 running at 33 MHz (486DX running at 33 MHz preferred)

- 6 MB of memory (16 MB preferred)

- 60 MB hard disk drive (300 MB plus preferred)

- tape or other storage device to create an image of the final multi-media application that can be sent for CD-ROM production

- audio board with minimum 8-bit DAC, linear PCM sampling, 11 and 22 kHz sampling rates (only necessary if your title will use sound)

- minimum 8-bit video card

- MS-DOS operating system 3.30 or higher

- a multi-session, multi-speed CD-ROM drive

- Microsoft Windows 3.1 or later

- Microsoft Word 2.0 for Windows or later is a recommended option.

This is the specification needed to create, or author, a multimedia title using Viewer 2.0. But a lower specification would allow you to view (or playback) the finished software. This would be a 16 MHz 386SX computer with 2 MB of memory, 30 MB hard disk drive, CD-ROM drive with a minimum one second data seek time, Windows 3.1 and a mouse. However, this would barely work and a more realistic minimum would be a 25 MHz 486SX processor and 4 MB of memory for the finished software to perform well.

Once installed Viewer 2.0 gives you a whole host of mini-applications that can be used for software development: the Viewer program, Viewer Gallery, Viewer Compiler, Project Editor, HotSpot Editor, WaveEdit, BitEdit, Convert, Media Player, Viewer API, Multimedia Authoring Guide, and PalEdit. Together these mini-applications give you just about everything you will need to create a multimedia application. However, what manifests itself when you first start using Viewer 2.0 is its complexity. It is not for the faint hearted. This development environment takes for granted that the user has been a programmer, with at least the Basic programming language, for several years, and understands an audio/video interleave (AVI) file format.

The only way to start creating an application with Viewer 2.0 is to run the Viewer Gallery application and start looking at all the components. View the Hypertext editor, search engine and the various Windows layouts that can be achieved using this software.

The development cycle starts with the Project Editor, and once started you should run the tutorial that ships with the software. This will take you through the entire process of starting your electronic book or entertainment software package. Again, this book is no replacement for the real thing so the only way to really get to grips with Viewer 2.0 is to use it.

Development with Viewer 2.0 is a very laborious process. The best way to get any real benefit from its mini-applications is for a team of people to work together on a multimedia application. There is an awful lot of repeating step 1 and step 2 in order to move onto step 3. Be patient with this software because the end results are well worthwhile.

A pet hobby of mine for many years now has been Science Fiction movies, of which I have a large collection. With Viewer 2.0 I managed to create an electronic guide to my 300 Sci-Fi movie collection with audio clips, images and text in just under three weeks. The task was not easy, and took a lot of sleepless nights to finish. Given more time and manpower directed at my particular task Viewer 2.0 would have produced a very professional looking multimedia application. Instead the software resulted in grey hairs overnight as I fought to combat its complexities.

Multimedia Viewer 2.0 is more of a programming tool than a multimedia authoring tool. It needs a fair amount of knowledge about the way that rich data types work and are created in order to be used. It is a powerful tool in the hands of an experienced programmer, or team of programmers.

But that's not what multimedia authoring tools are all about. The really powerful ones are the software packages that do all the hard work for you, but unfortunately, they are few and far between. There is a wide variety of packages on the market, but not that many actually fulfil this requirement.

Until recently much of the software on the market was difficult to use, expensive, and limited in its options. Most software required a user to have a level of programming ability, be it in Basic or C/C++, to fine tune the multimedia software. Not everybody has this ability which is why the software is limited to the experts.

Microsoft did take the Windows programming world out of the dark ages and into the 1990s with the programming language Visual Basic (VB). Although VB is not for complete novices anybody can learn to use it within a few weeks of reading the manuals.

# Adobe Premiere

More recently, Adobe launched Premiere for Windows which is among the most complete, and easy to use authoring tools on the market. Much of this remaining chapter will concentrate upon what this application can do. It is one of the best development tools on the market.

First, this software needs a high powered computer to make it work: it will not run on anything less than a PC with 8 MB of memory, and its documentation goes as far as to recommend 32 MB for optimum performance. Having plenty of memory in your machine is essential when it comes to running Premiere. Although the software will run in 8 MB its performance is severely hampered, even on a computer with a large disk cache.

The software will run on a machine configured with a standard 8-bit 256 colour VGA card with a resolution of 640 × 480. But a 16- or 24-bit video card will allow more colours to be displayed, and as these cards are normally accelerated for use under Windows they will greatly enhance performance.

As with other aspects of multimedia a lot of hard disk space is needed, and Premiere needs up to 80 MB. Not all of this is taken up with program files, but the software has a tendency to run out of memory, so it temporarily stores data on the disk and then retrieves it when it wants it.

A feature of Windows is its ability to use the hard disk as memory. This is known as virtual memory and is used when all the RAM is used up by a program. There are no real hard and fast rules about how to set up virtual memory on a PC, other than to say that it is not as fast as memory chips so do not rely upon it. If you do your applications will run slowly.

However, let's assume that we cannot afford 16 MB of memory and our budget only allows for a machine running Premiere with a mere 8 MB. There are ways of helping the performance of the software by scrutinising the way Windows is set up.

First, you can limit the size of the Windows disk cache by adjusting the memory allocation of the SMARTDRV.EXE utility. This program works by reserving memory into which commonly used data on your hard disk is stored.

This is not a problem when you have lots of memory, but when you have a machine with 8 MB of memory you should really only allocate about 512 KB. SMARTDRV.EXE automatically defaults to a setting of 2 MB on a machine with 8 MB of RAM, so after installing Premiere always check your system to make sure you haven't lost memory to this utility. Full information on adjusting the memory settings of SMARTDRV.EXE can be found in the Windows manual.

Another useful tip, and this goes for other applications as well, is always to start Adobe Premiere before any other application. This guarantees that Premiere has access to all Windows resources and memory. If you don't the Adobe program will be forced to fight other software for Windows memory and this will inhibit perfor-mance.

Windows can be forced to load a program directly from the DOS prompt before it performs any other system tasks. This is achieved by typing the default WIN command and the name of the program you want to run with a space in between them. With Premiere, you would type WIN PREMIERE. This command is of course available to any other Windows program so if you wanted to auto start Windows with its word processor you would type WIN WRITE.

If after making both these changes Premiere still runs slowly on your machine then it may be a good idea to check your WIN.INI file and the Windows StartUp Group. Delete any unnecessary start up items in order to give the software more memory. Be careful when performing this task because you may delete an important command that stops Windows from running. It is probably a good idea to copy the WIN.INI file to a floppy disk before making the changes just in case of any problems.

Once installed, Premiere displays a simple screen with what can only be described as a workbench area (see Figure 6.2). This screen area holds a record of all the data files currently in use and a view of the new multimedia application currently under development.

The idea of Premiere is to make a 'movie', and this can be achieved by taking real time images from a camera, VCR, professional tape deck or by using pre-stored images which are commonly sold on compact disk. Premiere is designed to support two video formats: Windows. AVI and Macintosh QuickTime.

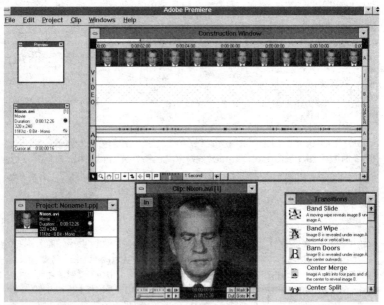

**Figure 6.2 The Adobe Premiere Edit screen can be used to construct multimedia movies**

Other images that can be used include screen shots, in TIFF or PICT format, and animation files with the .FLC or .FLI extension can be used. All of these images can be strung together and then a digital audio sound track can be added as a finishing touch.

The software is easy to use and revolves around the concept of a person working on a project and developing a collection of multi-media clips that are organised along a time line. The sequence of events goes something like this:

1. Start a new project and load into memory the multimedia data clips you want to use.

2. View the clips to see how long they are or how large and then arrange them on the time line.

3. You can use a construction window to view all the data in case you change your mind.

4. You can add a wide variety of transitions and filters to the assembled clips which determines how they will be faded together, and gives a professional touch to the movie,

5. Once you think you are happy with the assembled data Premiere allows you to preview the movie.

6. Compile the finished result into one single data file, most commonly a Video for Windows file. This file presents itself as a movie which can be viewed on any machine running Windows.

Of course, this sequence of events is not set in stone and will no doubt depend upon the type of multimedia data you intend to use. For example, the finished result of your labours may not be a Video for Windows file, but a video output to a VCR. In this case a complete understanding of the various hardware add-ons to your machine is essential and this will no doubt impact upon the sequencing of a movie.

Premiere comes with a useful set of help files and teaching files designed to take a novice and turn them into a video editing genius. But be patient. Mastering the software does take time: you can't expect to be the digital equivalent of Renoir over night. As you grow to understand the software so you will discover new talents that were previously hidden.

Although Premiere is capable of producing really high quality video sequences it is a big mistake to try to be too clever with all this technology. Just because there are many features at your disposal, do not try to use them all in one sequence. Clever effects mixed with dull material do not make a good video. There are times when using a clever fade or dissolve (and Premiere's got plenty of these), will do little more than make boring material interesting. So choose your materials well and give your projected audience credit for actually digesting the material and not just the neat effects.

# —— Animation Works Interactive ——

Cartoons can be fascinating, enjoyable and funny to watch. As you know a cartoon is made up of a series of single images viewed consecutively as an animation. Companies like Walt Disney have made a fortune pampering to the delights of children and adults with high quality animations like Aladdin and Jungle Book, as well as with numerous cartoon characters. However, the history of animation goes back to the very early days of the Egyptian murals when figures were depicted, carved in stone, forming a variety of tasks. Vases from ancient Greece, and early Japanese scrolls have all depicted animation, albeit in the crudest form of a series of drawings.

Now I'm not saying that we can all make our own animated cartoons in the same mould as Disney, but what we can do is add an element of fun to the world of multimedia with custom animations.

The US software company Gold Disk has put together various tools that allow you to create animations under the single title of Animation Works Interactive. This software package will work on a machine with as little as 2 MB of memory and requires only 5 MB of free disk space to store each working file. Optional technology used by this software includes a sound card and a CD-ROM player, although neither are requirements in the animated world.

Animation is not easy, and is a great deal harder to implement than digitising a video sequence. After all, with video, the source images have already been created and all you are doing is capturing them. Animation requires artistic input if it is to look professional.

An animation is created principally in three steps. At the beginning you need to design the object, or actor, that is to be animated. Next you have to create a background, and finally you assemble both elements into the animated movie. Animation Works Interactive provides all the tools you need to complete these three steps (see Figure 6.3).

First you have to decide on the background you want for your animation. This can be a background specific to the animation, such as a sea bed for animated fish, or it may well be a still image captured from a camera, or even a video sequence over which an animation is being played.

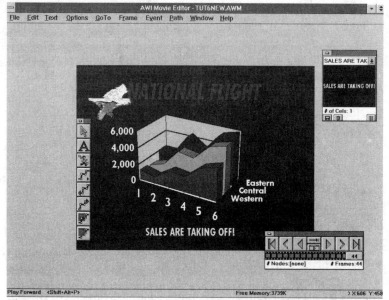

**Figure 6.3  Animation Works Interactive has been used to liven up spreadsheet data**

The software comes with a utility called Background Editor which is basically a 256 colour paint program that can read .GIF, .DIB, and .BMP files and can output .DIB bitmap files. This means that you can use any other paint program to make or edit your backgrounds, provided that it supports one of these three image formats.

The next utility is the Cel (*sic*) Editor, which is used to create the various single images of an actor to be put together to form an animation. This utility offers similar drawing options to the Background Editor, but its main emphasis is on sequencing images.

Professional animators draw each component of their actors on tracing paper and during the process of drawing, continually flip from one page to another to check that an animation is working. Animation Works uses a similar technique, called onion skinning to allow the designer to track the animation. When turned on, this feature allows the software to display a thin image of the previous or next cell on top of which the current cell being edited can be drawn. This allows for comparisons to be made at each stage of an animation, enabling a smooth finish to be achieved.

The final program, and the heart of Animation Works, is the Movie Editor. This program does the hard bit – blending actors into the background. Together these three utilities allow a wide variety of animated effects to be used to create anything from a man walking across the screen to an aeroplane landing on an aircraft carrier.

Having said all of this, it's not easy. Animation demands artistic skills, and not all of us can become Walt Disney overnight. Animation Works Interactive is one of the best packages in its class and when mastered can be used to create stunning animations.

# Asymmetrix Compel

In the opening chapter I discussed the various business applications that can benefit from multimedia, and this included presentation graphics packages. Sometimes it might not seem like it but there is an art form behind designing business slides.

Asymmetrix is a software company closely affiliated to Microsoft, so close that both were founded with the help of a man called Paul Allen. Asymmetrix was founded around a product called Toolbook, which is a programming environment designed to help Windows users develop Windows applications more quickly. Following the success of Toolbook the company launched Compel, a presentation graphics package which has multimedia at its heart. This package is built from the ground up with the ability to use sound, animation, clip art and video sequences to help a presenter create a presentation that leaves A4 flip charts in the dark ages.

Designed to run on a 386 or higher PC (preferably 486 running at about 33MHz) Compel needs 2 MB of memory (4 MB recommended) and costs $295. A compact disk player and sound card are not required but obviously would make things a lot better.

But what exactly is a presentation? It is a visual aid designed to help convey a message to an audience via slides. These slides can be delivered via a computer screen or an overhead projector, bearing in mind that not many people can crowd around a computer monitor.

Standard presentation graphics software such as Microsoft PowerPoint, Lotus Freelance and Harvard Graphics are designed mainly to deal with standard paper based text presentations, which are then turned into overhead foils. Multimedia data can be used by these packages but support has been added as more of an afterthought rather than an integral part of the application.

Compel's strength, and weakness is that its forte is multimedia and not paper based handouts or overhead foils. Asymmetrix claims that Compel removes the need to employ a graphics artist and that any user of a computer can make multimedia presentations using its software. This is both an accurate and inaccurate statement.

It is true to say that the novice can use the tools within Compel to make a business presentation that deafens an audience with stereo sound effects and blinds them with stunning visuals. But the novice will undoubtedly fall foul of the one simple task that Compel is supposed to perform: that of presenting information.

Compel makes it so easy for a user to add sound and video to a presentation that nine times out of ten you find yourself worrying about where a video clip is located on the screen or how long a sound clip plays for, forgetting to present the text information that the package is supposed to do.

Having said all this the software is easy to use and the results that can be achieved when using it are remarkable. Unlike many other software packages on the market Compel makes it so easy to work with multimedia data you think you had been born to it.

# Macromind Action!

One of the best selling multimedia packages is Macromind Action! which is a rival to Compel, although there are several subtle differences.

Action! is able to take a static image, such as an overhead projector slide show, and to bring it to life, not necessarily with video or stereo sound effects, but with animations of text and pictures. It can take the static text that is at the centre of a slide show and spin it around, flip it over, or dissolve it off the page and replace it with another sentence. Action! claims to add the dimension of time to a presentation in that events can be timed to go off during a slide show. These events can be automated by the computer or sequenced by the press of a mouse button.

A wide variety of painting tools is included with Action!, the majority of which are designed to add custom effects to text information. But as with Compel, the information in the presentation is there to assist you, and not the other way around. You are the star of a presentation, multimedia or not. A presentation will go no where if you leave the audience to understand the information represented on slides. They are to be used to prompt you about what you say next, with the multimedia data there to keep the audience awake and to add another dimension to the presentation.

# 7

# -VIDEO FOR WINDOWS-

In Chapter 5 we discussed the hardware add-ons that will make motion video possible with the average PC. In this part of the book we will look at the software that brings this hardware to life. Video for Windows is another Microsoft product that has now become the *de facto* standard for capturing and then displaying a video clip on several computers. With a price tag of £99 this software is the ultimate addition to the Windows operating system and complements the Multimedia Control Interface (MCI) control panel introduced in Windows version 3.1. Many video capture board suppliers bundle Video for Windows with their products, so check with them before buying.

Video for Windows brings with it the ability to mix and match video and audio – commonly called interleaving – to create a file format called audio/video interleave (.AVI). The software sequences the audio and video signals to make movies and assigns the .AVI file extension. The package includes a CD-ROM of video clips as well as installation disks. Once installed, Video for Windows adds a set of drivers to the MCI panel of Windows 3.1 and can then add support for a variety of video capture boards, such as the Intel SmartVideo board. Other hardware generally offers its own support for Video for Windows.

The two important programs included in Video for Windows are VidCap and VidEdit which make the hardware work. Figure 7.1 shows what VidCap and VidEdit look like. At the top of VidCap are a menu bar and the tool bar, with the video capture screen in the middle and the status bar at the bottom. The menu bar gives users access to the various options that can be changed to alter video capture sequences. This includes the audio capture format, video format, video source, video display, preview video mode and overlay video mode.

The SmartVideo board does not provide direct audio support so the board relies on drivers installed for a sound card to capture audio and then sequence it with a video image. Audio support is provided for both 8- and 16-bit sound and a sample rate from 11.025 to 44.100 kHz. The option of mono and stereo support is also available.

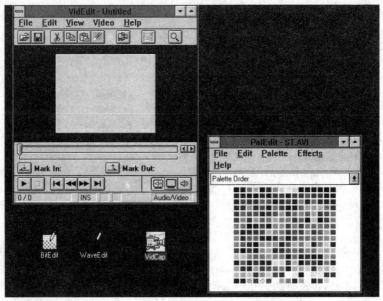

Figure 7.1  Video for Windows offers an array of editing tools

# Using VidCap

Next you need to think about the video source that will be captured by Video for Windows. It can take in a direct RGB (i.e. red, green and blue) video image, composite image and S-Video picture, in either a NTSC or PAL standard. In addition to these settings the hue, saturation and contrast levels of a picture can be modified. After these settings have been made Video for Windows allows the size of an image to be changed and the colour depth to be adjusted. As stated before the image size affects the size of the captured video file and also affects the quality of the captured image.

The colour depth control has the greatest effect on storage requirements. In standard 8-bit mode, up to 256 colours per pixel can be allocated for every video frame. In 16-bit video mode this changes to 32 767 colours assigned per pixel without a palette being attached and in 24-bit mode this figure becomes 16 000 000 colours per pixel without a palette. However, these settings double and treble the storage requirements of a file compared with an 8-bit colour depth.

The default setting for VidCap is to grab an image with an 8-bit colour depth using a single palette. The default palette is a basic 64-shade grey scale, although the black and white video sequences can be improved using one of two methods.

The first method is to supply your own palette to VidCap before grabbing a video sequence, and the second is to change the video format to 16- or 24-bit, which will then assign a full colour palette to VidCap automatically. The former is the best option for most video work because it allows you to keep file sizes to a minimum by only working in 8-bit mode. The latter doubles or quadruples the data size.

A palette can be supplied by capturing the existing palette of one or more frames from a video sequence, or by loading a palette from an external picture, such as a bitmap (.BMP), or from a palette file with a .PAL extension. Getting the palette right is a tricky operation and there is no substitute for experimentation. The right palette will dramatically improve the quality of a captured image, but the palette of choice will change from one source device, such as a VCR or camera, to another.

Once you have managed to set the VidCap colour palette then you can start worrying about several other options: frame rate, capture time limit, capture audio, capture to memory and capture to disk.

The frame rate is critical to the overall capture of a video file. There is more detail about this in Chapter 4.

The capture time limit is a setting that controls VidCap by saying that 10, 15 or more seconds of video will be captured and saved before the software stops accepting any more images. How long this capture period might be is determined by the physical limitations of memory and hard disk space.

Before video is captured Video for Windows needs to know whether the video clip will be stored in memory prior to being saved or stored in a disk cache specially created by the software. You need to know how much memory your PC has before you make this calculation.

If you have 16 MB of system memory you will be able to capture about 40 seconds of video before the data stream stops. Having 32 MB of memory will allow almost two minutes of video to be captured without a problem. Capturing into memory is the most efficient way of ensuring that a video clip is of high quality and perfectly synchronised with its audio.

Capturing to a hard disk is probably the cheapest way of collecting a video clip. It is possible to make VidCap grab a video sequence as large as the spare space on the disk drive. The only problem with this is that a high speed disk drive, such as a SCSI-II or fast IDE, is needed if every frame in a sequence is to be captured. Slow drives can lead to 'dropped frames' which will diminish the quality of the finished clip. Capturing direct to memory will stop this phenomenon happening, but not everybody has a massive amount of memory. A fast hard disk will, if well looked after, also operate without dropping frames.

You can also help the situation by thinking carefully about the video source before capturing it. The more help that you give a PC during the process of capturing a video clip the better. The following tips will help capture smaller uncompressed files which will reduce the load on a computer, both at the time of capture and later playback:

- Always try to minimise the amount of data that changes between each frame. This can be achieved by capturing images on a static landscape which will allow you to produce excellent compression ratios. For example, avoid panning or zooming a camera while shooting a video clip as this will lower the compression ratio which is not good.

- When capturing colourful images try to go for ones that are constant in their colour and not fine grained. When capturing backdrops you should select a solid colour and not textured areas.

## Edit away

Once an image has been captured it must then be worked upon by VidEdit. The VidCap utility does not compress or interleave data in the captured video clip. This must be performed by VidEdit. In its uncompressed form the video will play but not very quickly.

The beauty of a captured video file is that it is stored on a hard disk in a contiguous portion of the disk which makes it easy to edit. It is a good idea always to keep a copy of the original captured file so that you can experiment using several compression and interleave options.

Every time you apply a different compression method to a video file it lowers the quality. So performing two compressions on the same piece of video, while experimenting with the options, will produce a low quality video image.

But the use of VidEdit goes further than just compressing a video clip. It can be used to extract shorter clips from within a larger video file and to then splice together several of these clips to form a custom sequence. By playing around with the interleave settings a video clip can be synchronised with its audio – or a completely separate piece of audio captured somewhere else – and then saved as a fully interleaved and compressed .AVI file.

VidEdit also has the ability to run more than one copy of itself which allows a number of video clips to be worked upon, which speeds up the overall video editing stage of Video for Windows.

This utility offers a variety of compression techniques which basically allow you to make trade-offs against the quality, size and compression time of a video sequence. Some compression methods do not store the full video information within each frame, but instead overlay information taken from the previous frame on top of the current frame being edited by VidEdit. This is fine when you are scrolling forward in a video clip to view what happens next because VidEdit can provide a complete image. However, this can cause problems when scrolling backwards because, when you jump forward to a frame, the images from the previous frame may not be available because that frame has not been stored with its full video information, so the frame you display will be incomplete. If this occurs VidEdit can be adjusted so that it corrects the problem by reconstructing the full-frame image by sequentially displaying the video data from any frame prior to the one being viewed. Unfortunately, this has a major effect on performance which is why VidEdit can be selected to operate at fast or full-frame update, giving you the choice of speed or accuracy.

The audio side of a video sequence is as important as the image being shown. There is no point running a video of somebody singing if you cannot hear their voice. VidEdit has a number of different audio settings ranging from crude mono, 8-bit, 11 kHz to 16-bit stereo with a capture frequency of 44 kHz.

Earlier in the chapter we talked about setting the colour palette so that a good quality capture can be achieved. In VidEdit this is moved one stage on as you are forced to start thinking about what sort of computer the video clip is to be played back on later. You may well have a high quality 24-bit, super bells and whistles graphics card but the average man in the street has not. If you plan to distribute a video clip once captured, perhaps as part of a game or an electronic book, then effort has to be put into making the palette accurate. Not enough emphasis is placed on palette editing, but this can be the difference between good quality video clips and trash.

Video for Windows demands a fast data transfer rate from the storage device you have used to save your video clip, through the I/O bus to the processor and then into the video and sound hardware. This sequence of events can lead to a strange number of anomalies occurring in a captured video sequence.

Say, for example, you are using a high powered machine for video capture, with 32 MB of memory and 1 GB of high speed SCSI II disk storage installed on a 32-bit local bus PCI slot, all driven by a 66MHz Pentium processor. When compressing video with such a computer you will have optimum data throughput, which allows VidEdit to perform its function at a high data transfer rate. Unless you are careful the finished video clip will also be optimised to work on this high specification alone. But the video may eventually be viewed on a machine with a much lower specification, perhaps with a CD-ROM player rather than a hard disk.

The data transfer rate of the storage device which holds a video clip is critical to just how smooth a video clip looks when it is displayed. If the video clip is mastered to load from a high speed 300 KB per second disk drive and is then displayed from a slow 150 KB per second CD-ROM drive problems will occur. Even moving an image from one computer to another can cause problems.

Common problems include a sort of 'warbling' effect on audio because it is not being synchronised with the video, or the same reason can cause audio to run ahead of the video clip. These are just some of the common problems that have to be dealt with when playing around with Video for Windows. Even with high quality software like Adobe Premiere, which performs most of the synchronisation of a video/audio clip for you, the running ahead effect can develop.

In the options menu of VidEdit there is a range of choices when it comes to the target storage device for a video clip. You will have to tinker with these settings to figure out which is best for you. The choices are:

- hard disk
- hard disk (interleaved)
- hard disk (300 KB/second)
- hard disk (150 KB/second)
- hard disk (100 KB/second)
- CD-ROM (150 KB/second)
- CD-ROM (80 KB/second)
- Custom

You can also choose to work with several different compression algorithms, and these include:

- no recompression
- full frames (uncompressed)
- Microsoft Video 1
- Intel Indeo Video Raw
- Intel Indeo Video R3.0
- Cinepak Codec by SuperMatch

These are just the basic settings that can be used to make sure that a video clip is compressed accurately. In the target device option, the custom selection is useful because it will allow you to cater for any storage hard disk you might be using, such as the specialised Micropolis AVI disks which are designed specially for storing digital video images on, or the new quad-speed CD-ROM players (see Chapter 9).

Microsoft has tried to make Video for Windows future proof by allowing it to use different software Codecs. Third parties can write their own Codecs which can be added to Video for Windows, such as the Cinepak software. As time goes by both Intel and Microsoft are updating and improving their respective Codecs which constantly improves the capture and compression of video clips.

# ——————— What's it all about? ———————

Video for Windows is an exciting package to use and when used properly it can be a powerful tool. The art of mastering this sort of program is constant use. You need to play around with it all the time and fine tune it to the multimedia equipment installed within your computer.

Each machine has its own performance problems. A fast video card and a fast video capture card will work well together and will no doubt result in high quality motion video clips being captured. But a video card of average performance, combined with a fast video capture unit will give different results.

This means that the settings for a capture card, such as a SmartVideo board, will need to be changed from machine to machine. Nothing is constant in the world of multimedia and this is what causes problems for end users.

Video for Windows is an 'open' product, in that it works on several software and hardware platforms, such as the Apple Macintosh, Modular Windows, Windows 3.1, Windows NT and future operating systems yet to be developed, and has what are called open APIs.

API stands for application programming interface and is a method by which other Windows software communicates with Video for Windows. Microsoft has made access to Video for Windows easy to third party software developers which is why the software has done so well.

Many games makers like Sierrra sell CD-ROM-based games with a run-time version of Video for Windows installed free of charge. This does not give people access to the editing tools which come with the complete version but does allow a person who buys a game with video sequences included, but does not own Video for Windows, to view the video clips. The runtime is royalty free and can therefore be distributed widely to a number of users.

One important issue concerning Video for Windows has nothing at all to do with the software. The source of the video information is critical. I would strongly recommend using an S-VHS video recorder, such as the Mitsubishi M1000, which outputs a high quality image in either composite or S-Video which every video capture board on the market supports. Other video sources include cameras and laserdisc players. There is much more about this in Chapter 4.

# 8

# WHAT MAKES A GOOD MULTIMEDIA PC?

In this chapter we will look at some standard Intel-based computers and discuss how these machines can be modified with various video and sound hardware so that they then comply with the Multimedia Personal Computer (MPC) standards committee guidelines (see Chapter 12). The following sections describe two computers that I have modified for multimedia and two that I have built. My experience with these computers should assist you in working out what you need to do to set up or buy your own multimedia computer.

## —— The Samsung SysteMaster ——

The first machine is several years old and manufactured by Samsung, the giant Korean computer and electronics maker. The SysteMaster 486/25TE is a full height tower computer based around the Intel 486DX chip running at 25 MHz and comes with a 32-bit EISA expansion bus. Although this machine was not made for multimedia work, being originally intended for use as a network file server, the SysteMaster 486/25TE is a beautiful machine for conversion into a multimedia PC.

This computer originally had 8 MB of memory and other standard features included 3.5 inch and 5.25 inch floppy disk drives, two 120 MB hard disk drives and a Trident VGA graphics card with 512 KB of video memory. This is a good specification for standard application work, but nowhere near what is needed for multimedia.

To the Samsung machine I added a Sound Blaster Pro 16-bit stereo sound card which comes with a non-standard SCSI interface (see Chapter 9) to which I attached a Matsushita CD-ROM player which has several internal audio connections. The CD-ROM drive fits into one of the remaining 5.25 inch expansion bays at the front of the Samsung PC, and even the colour schemes match.

Installation of both the sound card and the CD-ROM player is very easy because the Samsung computer has a lot of free space inside it. This is an important feature with a PC because with multimedia comes a host of lovely cables that need to be connected from one expansion card to another. The 16-bit expansion card, which caters for both sound and the CD-ROM drive, resides in a single slot inside the Samsung tower PC. It is secured using a single screw and has two cables which attach to the CD-ROM player. One carries audio data and the other carries data from a CD into the PC's memory.

For the two new devices to work a software device driver for each needs to be installed. Creative Labs, the creators of the Sound Blaster Pro, have made the installation of the card and CD-ROM player very easy. The installation software automatically checks the hardware and memory settings for the sound card, to ensure that it is working, and then installs the DOS drivers, which initialise the hardware when the computer is first switched on, and then install Windows utilities.

The Creative Labs solution is a neat and easy to install sound/CD-ROM add on kit. The best part of the deal is the Sound Blaster Pro card which is one of the best sound cards on the market and supported by just about every multimedia application or game on the market. The CD-ROM drive is neat in design but is not the fastest on the market. It has a transfer speed of around 152 KB per second which is average to say the least.

After installing a few multimedia applications – Compel, Toolbook, Adobe Premiere and so on – I quickly discovered that 240 MB of disk storage was inadequate, so I upgraded the system with a bigger 340 MB Western Digital hard disk. I installed this as the boot disk, and then added a SCSI-II controller card to which I attached an optical disk drive for archiving data.

The next upgrade performed on the SysteMaster 486/25TE was to replace the Trident graphics board with an ATI Technologies Mach32 board, which is very fast, displays several million colours, and generates a crisp high resolution picture. It is optimised to work with Video for Windows.

To recap, the Samsung tower now has a CD-ROM drive, 460 MB of online data storage, a 16-bit sound card, accelerated graphics card and a massive archive storage unit. So what else is needed? A video capture board, and this is where the fun started.

Having paid out for one of the first DVA-4000 cards several years ago I was disappointed when it failed to work in my Samsung. In fact, the card refused to work with any of my other PCs but more about this later. So I tried the Intel SmartVideo Recorder in the Samsung and it also failed to work. What I did manage to get working was the Videologic Captivator board and the upgraded Videologic MediaSpace system which features a new DVA-4000 motion video card. With this, the Samsung PC was fully equipped as a multimedia delivery computer.

The only problem with the computer was that the 25 MHz 486DX chip showed itself to be too slow for multimedia capture work. So a 486DX2 chip replaced the 25 MHz 486DX chip and almost doubled the performance of the system. This is a much quicker chip and complements multimedia work.

So now the Samsung had all the multimedia hardware I needed, and apart from the problems with video capture boards the operation was relatively simple, but getting the software right was a nightmare. My software problems were not caused by the Samsung hardware, but by a generic problem with multimedia software drivers.

Each software driver loaded into a computer's memory eats away at the 640 KB of conventional memory on the computer. When the Samsung was first turned into a multimedia PC I was running MS-DOS 5.0 which is not the easiest version of DOS with which to configure memory. So I turned to the Qualitas 386MAX version 6.0 memory manager. On the Samsung this utility appeared to free up most of the base 640 KB of memory, but appeared to work when it felt like it. The software demonstrated the unfortunate ease with which Windows can crash when running multimedia software.

On more occasions that I care to remember Windows 3.1 bombed out when I ran a sound edit program or a video edit tool. It sometimes seemed that Windows was working against me. I couldn't understand this because the hardware was perfectly set up and working well. The whole problem arose from memory conflicts caused by Windows 3.1 and 386MAX.

After upgrading to MS-DOS 6.0 and then version 6.2 I decided to scrap 386MAX and move to using the Microsoft MemMaker memory manager. This appeared to fix the problems with a lot of the system crashes. Either that, or I got so used to the computer crashing every time I ran a multimedia program that I stopped noticing and simply took it for granted.

# The Apricot Xen LSII

Apricot Computers, probably one of oldest PC makers still operating in the UK, was one of the first PC makers to move towards adding stereo sound support to its PCs as standard.

The company's Xen LS II desktop computer has the Business Audio hardware – co-developed by Compaq and Microsoft – integrated onto its motherboard. With its integrated network support and small desktop size the Apricot machine is ideal as a multimedia playback PC, but not as a development tool. Due to its small size the Xen PC only has two expansion slots – compared with the eight that the Samsung SysteMaster 486/25TE has to offer – which means that a limited number of expansion boards can be added.

As part of the Business Audio support Apricot has included a MIDI/joystick adapter, a microphone input and a speaker output. A volume control is located on the front of the computer, although it can also be software controlled from within Windows 3.1. The Business Audio chipset on the Xen's motherboard is completely Windows 3.1 compatible but is lacking when it comes to supporting DOS applications. Some games will work with the audio chips, but many do not.

Also integrated into the motherboard of the computer is a CD-ROM interface which allows for a Sony drive to be added. This can be easily installed, in a matter of minutes, and fits into a single drive bay at the centre of the machine. The drive can be hidden behind a moulded door and accessed when needed. As with any other CD-ROM drive the Sony model needs a special driver to work and this has to be installed manually. A major oversight by Apricot is to leave the software installation of the CD-ROM drive up to the PC owner, and not to automate it. But this is not that difficult a task if you follow the instructions.

This particular Xen LS II has 16 MB of memory and a 250 MB hard disk drive. All in all this is a pretty good specification which makes the Xen a good edit and playback machine, but weak as a development machine.

So the machine has a CD-ROM interface and stereo audio support without using up any of the two expansion slots. All you need to add is a video capture board and away you go. This is easier said than done.

Again my problems started when I tried to add a video capture board to the PC. The first card I tried was the Intel Real-Time Video (RTV) delivery board. The RTV is an expensive, and technically advanced video card that not only captures images but uses hardware acceleration to improve video playback. But not on the Apricot Xen. I couldn't get it to work. There was always a hardware address clash which prevented the board from working. But this was not the only problem with the Xen because the model in my possession has a significant hardware problem.

Video images are synchronised and merged on a PC via the video feature connector. On most PCs this connector is wired conventionally, but not on the Xen. Two of the pins on the connector are wired a different way around which makes it impossible for a video card to interface with the Xen PC. This only became apparent after trying and failing to install the Intel RTV card. Then I read the Xen manual in full and discovered that you need to contact Apricot for a special feature connector which is wired differently to normal cables. Admittedly Apricot did mention this problem in the manual but I failed to spot it.

This problem has now been rectified in newer versions of the Xen LS II computer but this did not help my situation. As well as having the feature connector wired the wrong way around the Xen also has a problem with the location of the feature connector on the motherboard. With a card installed in an expansion slot the connector socket is difficult to locate and then fit a cable into.

The next video card I tried to install was the Intel SmartVideo board which also failed to work in the computer. Even with the help of an Intel technical engineer I could not get the card working. Repeated phone calls to Apricot also failed to rectify the technical problem.

The only video capture card I could get running was the Videologic Captivator board. This worked first time and continued to run without any problems.

The Xen posed a number of problems when it came to multimedia software, not least in the area of memory. The machine implements an unusual memory architecture which means that a lot of the base 640 KB is consumed by drivers, with software like MemMaker and 386MAX failing to win it back.

With such a small computer, there is little room inside the Xen. As well as not working in the Xen, the Intel RTV board failed to fit properly. When inserted into a slot the board flexed which left me feeling uncomfortable. When in use the RTV board heats up and will flex enough without the help of an expansion slot that is too short and flexes even more. This constant heating up and cooling down puts enough stress on an expansion board without the actual physical stress of a slot that is too short.

The Apricot looks on the surface to be the ideal machine to build into a multimedia workstation. The integrated audio and CD-ROM interfaces are useful, but the odd architecture of the Xen makes it a troublesome machine to use for multimedia. As a standard business PC you cannot go far wrong with the Xen but multimedia is not its forte.

I suspect the problems stem from integrating all the components on the motherboard which force memory addresses and hardware interrupts to be pre-allocated. Multimedia hardware needs a wide range of floating hardware interrupts in order to prevent problems.

This sounds negative, and given the time and experience of an Apricot technical support engineer everything I have mentioned can be fixed. But engineers do not grow on trees.

# —— Building a desktop computer ——

There is an old saying that if you want something doing properly do it yourself. So during the research of this book I decided to make my own PCs that I would then turn into multimedia development machines.

I opted to build two computers: one in a desktop case with eight expansion slots and one in a large floor standing tower case with lots of room for expansion. So let's look at the building of the desktop system first.

The motherboard I chose to build the computer around cost a little over £100 and came with three high performance Vesa VL local bus expansion slots. The remaining five slots are standard 16-bit ISA. The motherboard can accommodate a variety of processor chips and I decided to use a 66 MHz 486DX2 chip. Aside from the Pentium chip this is the fastest processor in the Intel family of processors.

Memory on the motherboard can be fitted in single in-line memory modules (or SIMMS) which come in 1 MB or 4 MB sizes. I opted for 16 MB because I needed high memory performance. The actual installation of the motherboard into the desktop case was simple and attaching power to it was a simple matter of following the instructions (even if half of them were in Korean and the rest in Chinese).

I decided to add a high performance AMI VL-based accelerator card that uses the Weitek Power 9000 graphics chipset. At the time of the research this was the best graphics silicon available and a bargain at its price of £350.

Once the graphics card was fitted it was time to think about the disk storage needs of the desktop system. A standard IDE controller is fine for most things, but for real high capacity storage I decided to add both a local bus IDE controller, with 32-bit disc caching, and a 32-bit Adaptec fast SCSI-2 controller. To the IDE controller I attached a 540 MB Western Digital Caviar IDE disc drive, and to the Adaptec SCSI-2 card I linked up a 1.2 GB Quantum SCSI disk drive.

With 1.74 GB of disk storage I felt safe to brave the deadly world of multimedia data.

The video system is suitably fast and stable and next came the choice of video capture board. After dabbling with the MediaSpace card from Videologic I opted to install the SmartVideo Recorder for its ease of use.

The process of building the PC took me less than an hour. The biggest problem with the building process came with the ridiculous LED display on the front which shows the speed, in megahertz, that the Intel processor is running at. A large number of jumper switches alternate the numbers shown in the LED panel and this is difficult to configure. In the end I settled for a machine that thought it was running at 150 MHz.

Adding the multimedia components – video capture card, sound card and video display card – was really easy.

This time, there were no problems in installing the hardware. A Sound Blaster Pro sound board was added.

For a CD-ROM player I opted to use an older drive from Hitachi, which falls well below the MPC specification for a CD drive (see Chapter 12). The decision to add the Hitachi drive was prompted by the simple fact that it was lying around. I also wanted to see if any multimedia data could be loaded from it. The answer to this is both yes and no, but see Chapter 9 for more information. The use of a Sound Blaster Pro card would easily allow a different CD-ROM player to be added later.

Next came the software installation. With MS-DOS 6.0 installed and Windows 3.1 with full multimedia extensions I hardly dented the 1.74 GB of storage, but I soon put paid to this. After installing my entire collection of 8-, 16- and 24-bit colour images I had eaten away just over 300 MB of hard disk. My audio file collection consumed 45 MB and then I loaded my .AVI files which ate a massive 500 MB of disk space. The rest of the storage capacity was taken up with applications and various Windows add-on files, such as 130 TrueType fonts.

Of all the machines on which I have installed multimedia hardware and software, this home-grown effort was both the easiest to configure and the fastest performer. This is the machine on the front cover of this book and its size makes it ideal for adding expansion cards.

The only problem that my handbuilt machine shared with the Apricot and Samsung machines is the issue of how much of the 640 KB base memory can be made free once the multimedia software device drivers have been installed. MemMaker soon sorted this out, which surprised me because it had failed to do so on the other two machines.

After five months of collecting multimedia software from a variety of sources I ended up with a PC fitted with 1.74 GB of hard disk that was full. Suddenly my massive storage capacity was gone and I had to do something about it. The 'fix' to my problem came in the form of a 1 GB Iomega external disk drive.

The LaserSafe Pro that I used is an optical disk drive which uses cartridges to store data. Each cartridge can hold 512 MB of data per side. The beauty of this type of device is the simple fact that when you want more storage all you have to do is eject the full one and insert a new blank one. Suddenly you have another gigabyte to fill. The capacity of this optical drive is superb and its data access time is, for an optical drive, excellent. The drive connects to a standard SCSI adaptor, such as the Adpatec which connects the Quantum drive, which means that the LaserSafe Pro can be connected to the computer without using another expansion slot.

All that needs to be added to the desktop PC are several software device drivers to make it work. The drivers extend the MS-DOS operating system so that it can read and write to a 1 GB optical disk drive. When installed, the drivers for the Iomega disk take up a lot of memory, which is a major problem. With the CD-ROM drivers, Quantum drivers and various DOS commands the all important first 640 KB of a PC's memory soon vanishes.

# —— Building a tower computer ——

Having built the desktop PC the next phase of the project was to put together the tower system. I decided to use the same motherboard and Intel processor as the desktop system. This machine was also equipped with 16 MB of memory, but this time I decided to stick with standard IDE disk drives. A 340 MB Western Digital drive and a 240 MB Samsung drive were added to this machine, which was also fitted with a 32-bit VL-based IDE cache controller card.

As an experiment I used the Microsoft DoubleSpace utility to compress the data stored on the 340 MB disk drive. This turned it into a drive with a capacity in the region of 700 MB, so in total this machine had just under 1 GB of storage. Because of the success of the Weitek Power 9000 card in the desktop machine, I installed the same card in the tower system. A significant improvement with this machine came with the addition of an external Toshiba CD-ROM drive.

The CD-ROM drive fitted was a multi-session triple speed unit which was Photo CD compatible. The data transfer speed of this drive is very fast making the Sound Blaster CD-ROM drive and the Hitachi drive look like they come from the dark ages.

Unusually I encountered a problem in making the VideoLogic MediaSpace card work in this machine. This was odd, because it worked in the desktop computer with exactly the same mother-board, so I once again had to resort to the trusted Intel Smart Video board.

Since I had run out of Sound Blaster Pro cards, this machine was equipped with one of the Microsoft Sound System boards. The only real problem with using the Microsoft card is that version 1.0 of the software that controls it has no support for DOS software. Version 2.0 has improved things, but even this lacks complete compatibility when it comes to running DOS games software.

Once configured this machine ran quickly but lacked performance because of its use of IDE drives. The addition of a SCSI-2 controller and a SCSI disk drive would have made a real difference to this computer, particularly when it came to capturing motion video images. But this technology is costly.

Chapter 5 mentioned the suspect reliability of disk compression software and on this tower machine the problem was encountered at the sharp end. After several weeks of use MS-DOS suddenly started reporting major errors with the data stored on the disk drive that had been compressed with DoubleSpace.

In the end I couldn't risk data loss so I was forced to re-format the disk without compression software and to add another disk drive to this computer. This was not however, an easy task. This machine was using an IDE controller which allows a maximum of two hard disks to be used at any time. Because I already had two drives installed I was forced to add a hard card.

A hard card is a disk drive which is bolted on to the side of a 16-bit expansion board and which fits into one of the slots on the PC's motherboard. The drive was a Quantum hard card with a 240 MB capacity. This solved my data storage problem and discouraged me from using data compression software.

It was unusual to notice the performance problems that multimedia software had on this tower computer because of the lack of SCSI disks. It reinforced an inherent problem with Windows 3.1 in that it relies far too much on storing data on a disk drive and not a PC's memory.

However, help was just around the corner in the shape of an upgrade to Windows 3.1 called Windows for Workgroups 3.11. An altogether faster version of Windows, version 3.11 has one major design improvement which helps multimedia no end: it has complete 32-bit file management subsystem. Even on a system with IDE drives this version of Windows really improves performance when capturing video sequences direct to a disk, and on a machine with fast SCSI disks capturing video to a disk drive becomes a pleasure and not a chore.

The Microsoft Sound System installed in the tower machine produces high quality stereo sound but it does have a few annoying features. To begin with, it has no manual volume control and in the Windows environment the volume is set via a utility program which you have to run every time you want to change the volume setting. This is annoying; with a Sound Blaster card there is a manual volume control that is easily accessible.

The incompatibility with DOS games, particularly multimedia DOS games eventually drove me to frustration with the Sound System. At one point I installed a second sound card and speakers just for use with DOS games.

It is worth noting though that for Windows use the Microsoft Sound System is one of the best cards on the market. It worked very well with all multimedia applications installed on the tower system and integrated extremely well with the Smart Video board, capturing high quality audio which could then be merged into an incoming video signal.

The real benefit of using a tower case is that is gives easy access to the expansion cards, disk drives and motherboard.

However, if you don't fancy making your own PC, and there are several reasons why you may not, there are many multimedia ready PCs on the market.

# 9

## CD-ROM

### The development of CDs

Digitally preserved in its plastic jacket the compact disk (CD) does not degrade, and because the music stored on it is digital, it is easy to interact with, making it ideal for use with computers.

Although CDs were initially developed for music use, they were soon adapted for use inside computers. The birth of the compact disc-read only memory (CD-ROM) came in the mid-1980s and brought with it a massive storage capacity. When the first CD-ROM drive was launched it offered hundreds of megabytes of storage at a time when many users where getting used to 1.44 MB floppy disk drives and 20 MB hard disk drives.

But why is the music-world CD called a CD-ROM when added to a computer? When a CD is made indentations are burnt into the polymer using a laser. The writing of data onto a CD is a one-way event: the data can never be changed. It becomes read-only memory (a computer term). Hence CD-ROM. The fact that CDs are read-only is a hindrance and has therefore led to their use as a reference medium.

Modern CD-ROMS can hold 600 MB of data, and they were used initially to store large amounts of text-based information. Later graphics and sound were added to CDs which was the beginning of CD-ROM becoming a critical component of multimedia.

The fact that CD-ROM is a read-only storage medium greatly reduces its use as a business storage device. This limitation does not, however, greatly affect its usefulness as a multimedia storage medium. In other chapters we have discussed that once a multimedia data file, such as a sound clip or video sequence, has been created it can then be archived for later use. This is where CD-ROM really comes into its own.

It is the ultimate archiving device and better yet, one of the cheapest. When it comes to distributing multimedia software, or for that matter any other software, a CD-ROM cannot be beaten. A master CD, from which any other is 'pressed', will cost £2–3000. This sounds a lot but when you take into account that each subsequent CD pressed from this master will cost well under £1, and perhaps as little as 55 pence, then the initial production costs become negligible if a reasonable number of CDs is to be manufactured. A CD can hold up to 650 MB of data. If this amount of software were to be distributed on 1.44 MB floppy disks, the cost would be many times higher.

One problem at the moment is that not everybody has a CD-ROM player for their computer. The world of Apple computers is more advanced than the PC community in that Apple is pro-actively marketing the advantages of multimedia and CD technology. The company is eager to persuade every Macintosh user to adopt CD-ROM technology and makes sure the technology is cheap.

For example, take the Apple PowerCD, which originally cost over £400, but which is now available for under £200. PowerCD is a three-way device. It can play CD-ROM software, traditional music CDs and a format invented by Kodak called Photo CD.

In the PC world the CD-ROM is growing in importance but its use is still limited. Depending upon whose market research you read there are 60–100 million Intel-based PCs in use worldwide, but only a small percentage of these machines are fitted with a CD-ROM drive. But this is changing. Many PC makers, such as Gateway 2000, Dell, AST, IBM, Compaq and many more are including CD-ROM drives in many of their systems at very competitive prices. For less than £2000 it is now possible to buy a Pentium computer system with a large hard disk and a good CD-ROM drive.

But what if you already have a PC and want to explore the world of CD-ROM? How do you choose which drive to buy?

## CD-ROM technology

When you are planning to buy a CD-ROM drive the first thing to look for is what type of connector links it into a host computer. The most basic CD-ROM drives have their own proprietary interface cards, usually 8- or 16-bit expansion cards. The problem with this sort of expansion card is that its only use is for connecting the CD-ROM drive. You cannot plug a scanner, printer or optical disc drive into the CD-ROM interface card. The good point about such a drive is that it generally comes in a kit form with all the software and cabling to set it up. Everything fits together, works and should not cause any problems when it comes to installation.

The most basic CD drives are called single-speed, single-session drives which are acceptable for DOS-based applications, but when it comes to new Windows software, such as Microsoft Cinemania these drives really start to struggle. I tested such a drive with Cinemania and the software informed me that the drive was too slow to run it, but it still allowed me to run the program. Cinemania is an advanced application that mixes stereo sound effects, high resolution still images and motion video clips. A single-speed drive can cope with the still images and audio, but struggles when it comes to motion video clips generated using Video for Windows.

For software such as Cinemania you need a fast drive with support for multiple sessions. Such drives are described as multisession and multispeed/multispin, CD-ROM drives. The multispeed CD-ROM drive came into existence with the NEC CDR-74 drive, but this type of CD-ROM drive is now widely available from many companies. The intense data requirements of most multimedia applications have forced the pace of CD-ROM drive development and the manufacturers have reacted with well priced products.

The basic principle of multispeed is to increase the data transfer rate of a CD-ROM drive by doubling the rotational speed of the disk. This means that a double speed drive will take the basic 150 KB per second transfer rate and double it to 300 KB per second. That's straightforward. But what about triple speed and quadruple speed drives? Do they work at 450 KB and 600 KB per second respectively? No.

It is not quite this simple. Different data stored on a CD are transferred into a computer at different speeds. CD audio for example is transferred at a slower rate than computer data. This means that a CD-ROM drive does not rotate at a standard speed, rather it speeds up and down as it deals with different data types. But this does not cause drive manufacturers too much of a problem and many now compensate for this varying speed using cache memory and so on.

Probably the most significant technology to hit the CD-ROM industry is the multisession CD, which allows a CD to be written to in more than one session. So what does this mean? Basically multisession technology allows data to be written to a CD again and again until it reaches its maximum 600 MB capacity. The whole issue of multisession comes into its own as various mixed media are recorded onto a CD.

Photo CD is perhaps the best example of a graphics technology that needs a multisession drive in order to work. If the CD-based software you buy is designated multisession, as Photo CD disks are, then only a multisession drive will be able to read them properly. A single session drive, such as the older Hitachi CDR-1600, will only be able to read the first recording of information on the CD and will miss the rest.

Multisession is a critical technology to have, and as time goes by and multimedia becomes even more complex then multisession drives will become more and more important. Think of the future when you buy a CD-ROM drive and I would recommend putting multisession, multispeed capabilities on your shopping list.

Remember that CDs can be scratched. They are not as indestructible as everyone would have you believe. On a music CD a scratch will result in a blip of noise that irritates you. On a CD holding computer software this scratch may well be the end of data, and therefore the end of the CD's usefulness.

There are two types of loading mechanisms for CD-ROM drives. Those with a tray loading mechanism are like audio drives, in that the CD is inserted on a tray, which then goes into the drive. The other type of drive uses a caddy. The CD is first placed in the caddy, which is then loaded into the drive. The advantage with the latter type of mechanism is that the caddy protects the CD from damage. This is a useful feature if you have any expensive CD-ROMs. Increasing numbers of drives, particularly the cheaper ones are tray-loading.

So, to reiterate the point. If you want a CD-ROM drive that meets the gruelling data access requirements of multimedia it has to support multiple sessions. Anything else just doesn't come up to scratch.

One of the best ways of connecting a CD-ROM drive to your computer is to buy a drive with a small computer system interface

(SCSI). This is a high speed interface which can transfer data at around 10 MB per second, which is more than enough for a CD-ROM drive. The SCSI interface is becoming more common in the PC world, not only because of its fast data transfer capability, but because a maximum of eight devices can be connected into each other and controlled by one single expansion card. This is achieved via 'daisy-chaining' cables from the back of a computer into the first device, such as an external CD-ROM drive, and then into the back of a scanner, optical disc drive and so on.

SCSI is a godsend to multimedia. It makes it very easy to mix and match external devices using a SCSI interface card, such as those made by Adaptec. The technology behind SCSI has also settled down meaning that when a device, such as a Toshiba CD-ROM, says it connects via a SCSI you are 99.9% certain that it will work with your other SCSI devices. And you only use up one PC expansion slot.

The third way to add a CD-ROM drive to a PC is to buy a sound card that comes with a SCSI connector as standard. However, the SCSI connectors on such sound cards do not support every SCSI drive on the market. Before buying always check with the supplier of the sound card for the recommended CD-ROM drive that goes with its card.

Westpoint Creative is a well known multimedia specialist operating in the UK. It is the UK reseller of equipment manufactured by a US company called Creative Labs which designed the very popular Sound Blaster sound card many years ago. Creative Labs uses a CD-ROM drive made by Panasonic which connects to the back of its Sound Blaster Pro 16-bit sound card. The two can be bought in a kit which includes the sound card, CD-ROM, cables, software and a bunch of multimedia programs: everything you need to get off the ground with multimedia. Chapter 8 describes how this kit was used to turn a Samsung computer into a multimedia PC.

This solution of boxing everything you need together makes a lot of sense. The hardware and software all works together and there should not be any installation problems. There are a number of companies that offer bundles, or multimedia upgrade kits, just like those from Creative Labs. The products range widely in terms of quality, cost and performance.

The simplest type of bare CD-ROM drive can cost you less than £150, although the more expensive drives cost up to £500. You can buy an internal drive, to go into a spare drive slot in your computer, or an external drive if your computer case does not have room for another drive, although these do cost more. There are also a few portable drives available.

Typical kits, with sound cards and, often, bundled CD-ROMs range from less than £300 up to £1000. These kits use drives from companies such as Sony, Toshiba, Panasonic, NEC and Mitsumi. If you have neither a CD-ROM drive nor a sound card, buying such a kit can be the cheapest way of acquiring both. It can also be the cheapest way of buying your first CD-ROM disks, but only if the CDs supplied are ones that you really want. Several retailers specialise in supplying multimedia hardware and software and it is worth looking in the computer magazines at what they have to offer.

Do remember though that you need at the very least to have a multisession Photo CD compatible dual speed drive, or even better one of the newer multispeed drives. When comparing the different drives, look at the access times and the data transfer rates. Access times are quoted in milliseconds (ms) and the fastest drives now have an access time of less than 200 ms, although a more typical access time would be around 300 ms. The smaller the number here, the better. Conversely, you should be looking for a data transfer rate that is as high as possible. A single speed drive will have a data transfer rate of 150 KB per second, while a double speed drive will be rated around 300 KB per second.

A selection of the kits available at the time of writing is described below. The comments made on these should help you determine what to look for.

## Media Vision Fusion CD 16

The Media Vision Fusion CD 16 is a CD-ROM bundle aimed at the low end of the computer market. As a consequence the bundle comes complete with a host of games software and the Philips CD-ROM drive included is neither multispeed nor multisession. If you want these two features the company offers a 'Professional' package at a higher price that does include a multisession, multispeed CD-ROM drive.

The 16-bit sound card included in the upgrade kit is pretty small and neat and has been carefully designed so that the analogue circuitry which produces the audio does not interfere with the digital chips fitted to the card.

A SCSI connector is standard on the edge of the sound card which allows the Philips LMSI CM 205 CD-ROM player to be attached. So the sound card and CD-ROM interface only take up one slot. The rear of the sound card has line-in, line-out, microphone and joystick sockets.

Although the sound card is shielded it is probably best fitted as far away from fax or video cards as possible. These cards often output a fair amount of interference and the delicate design of sound cards can pick up this interference, degrading sound quality.

The Philips drive is a single session, single speed 150 KB per second unit. Although the drive will work with Windows 3.1 and the majority of multimedia software on the market its lack of performance does limit any system it is installed in. So don't expect to watch any Photo CD discs on this unit.

CD-based software in the Fusion CD 16 bundle includes *Mantis, Civilisation*, the Deluxe Edition of *Where in the World is Carmen Sandiego?, Compton's Multimedia Encyclopaedia* and *Battle Chess*.

The best feature of this bundle is its ease of installation. Plenty of length on cabling allows for quick fitting and the software drivers, for DOS and Windows, are easy to set up. It is a nice entry level multimedia upgrade kit.

## NEC Multimedia Gallery

NEC is one of the world's leading makers of music CD and computer CD-ROM equipment so it is no surprise that the company offers a CD-ROM bundle.

The NEC Gallery is designed around the once top of the range NEC Multispin 74 CD-ROM drive, the first CD-ROM drive with a double speed spin which allowed the drive to transfer data at a rate of 300 KB per second. The Multispin 74 has a 64 KB cache and 280 ms access time which allow the drive to perform very well. Since its introduction the Multispin 74 has been usurped by a large number of CD-ROM drives and its 300 KB speed is nothing special. Having said this it is quite acceptable for most multimedia use.

The NEC Gallery multimedia system includes a Media Vision 16-bit sound card, speakers and software, but it is not cheap.

However, the software bundle that comes with Gallery to some extent makes up for the high price. You get the *New Grolier Multimedia Encyclopaedia, Mavis Beacon Teaches Typing*, Deluxe Edition of *Where in the World is Carmen Sandiego?*, *Great Wonders of the World Volume I, Guinness Disc of Records* and *Sherlock Holmes Consulting Detective*.

## Sony Desktop Library

Unlike many multimedia upgrade kits the Sony Desktop Library is made up almost exclusively of Sony equipment: the CD-ROM drive, speakers and even the CDs all carry a nice Sony logo, although the sound card is a 16-bit Spectrum card.

The kit takes up two expansion ports in a PC: one for the CD-ROM interface card and one for the audio card. Although this is not a huge problem it is inconvenient to waste two slots where one card could quite easily do the job.

You can choose between the CDU 31 LLL internal drive option, or the CDU 7305 external drive system. Again, neither is cheap.

The Sony drives included in these kits are only single speed 150 KB, multisession units which are adequate for the job of reading the CD titles bundled together, but not that hot for really intensive multimedia tasks. For example, I would not recommend running a Video for Window disk from these drives. Although they will read video data held on a CD-ROM, a drive with a 300 KB access time is really needed. The drives are through multisession which allows them to read and display Photo CD images.

Software is an essential part of a multimedia upgrade kit and Sony has put together a marvellous selection with its Desktop Library. You get the *New Grolier Multimedia Encyclopaedia, 1991 Time Magazine Compact Almanac, Tempra, Great Wonders of the World Volume I,* Deluxe Edition of *Where in the World is Carmen Sandiego?, The Presidents, Mavis Beacon Teaches Typing* and Photo CD sampler.

# Exeq LC

The Exeq is another multimedia upgrade kit based around the Sony CDU 31 CD-ROM drive. The kit is pretty basic but has a reasonable price tag. The documentation located in the kit looked at during the research for this book was pretty poor, consisting of nothing more than a pamphlet. But the kit is easily installed and also uses the now common Media Vision Spectrum 16 stereo sound card.

The hardware side of the kit is average but where Exeq LC really falls down is in the poor selection of software bundled with the hardware. All you get is a Kodak Photo CD sampler, *King's Quest V* and two electronic magazines from Nautilus and Nimbus.

## Unica Multimedia Upgrade Kit

On most CD-ROM drives a platter is ejected, you lay a CD on top and the drive then swallows it up. Not so with the Mitsumi drive that ships as part of the Unica kit. With this kit the whole CD-ROM drive pops out, you lift a lid, put a CD in and push it shut. Although rather odd the drive is effective and the design grows on you.

The Unica Multimedia Upgrade Kit is one of the best priced kits on the market. You get an internal CD-ROM drive that is double speed, multisession and transfers data at 300 Kbyte per second. For a little more, you can buy an external model with the same technical specification.

The software bundle included in the kit is fairly average: *Sherlock Holmes Consulting Detective, Hutchison Encyclopaedia* and *Hot Stuff*. The last CD is rather nice and is full of flashy multimedia demonstration programs, including MIDI files, digitised speech, animations and video clips, but it isn't that much use.

Unica has chosen to connect its CD-ROM drive into a PC via a Sound Blaster 16 16-bit sound card. Only one slot in the PC is taken up, which is good news for those with limited expansion options.

## WinStorm CD-ROM

The WinStorm was the most expensive multimedia upgrade kit looked at during the research of this book.

The 16-bit stereo sound card included in this kit is also a 24-bit graphics accelerator card bolted together and complete with 1 MB of video memory. The sound circuitry of the WinStorm card can sample 8-, 12- and 16-bit audio and the video circuits are capable of creating a 24-bit 640 × 480 pixel image, or an 8-bit 1,024 × 768 pixel image.

Earlier I mentioned how a sound card seated next to a video card could lead to interference problems. The makers of WinStorm appear to have done their jobs well because there are no problems with the audio playback of this card. The sound circuitry appears to be well shielded, which protects it from any interference.

The CD-ROM drive supplied with the WinStorm kit is a high performance NEC 55JD which is multispeed, multisession and transfers data at around 300 KB per second. The NEC drive is a real performer and ideal for just about any multimedia application. When video files were pulled off this drive there was no stutter effect, the playback was smooth.

This package is aimed squarely at the professional user, in that it could cost as much as many of the computers it is bought to fit into. Having said this, the WinStorm is well made and is a joy to use.

The software bundled with the package is also well selected: Animation's *MCS Musicrack*, Midisoft's *Multimedia Music Library*, Kodak Photo CD, the Deluxe Edition of *Where in the World is Carmen Sandiego?*, Asymetrix *Multimedia Make Your Point* and *Compton's Multimedia Encyclopaedia*.

# Photo CD

Earlier in the chapter I mentioned Photo CD. This is a technology developed by Kodak that was aimed primarily at the consumer world. The idea behind this technology is that we do away with all those photographs that get ripped and lost. Instead we go on holiday, take several hundred boring snaps of people on beaches and then have them 'printed' onto a CD. Then a Kodak Photo CD player can be plugged into your television set and used to view your holiday snaps.

The success of this technology is difficult to measure, but has almost certainly failed to accomplish its purpose so far and looks unlikely to replace the old fashioned paper photograph, but it does have several interesting uses when it comes to computers and multimedia. This is why many CD-ROM drive makers have built the capability to read Photo CD images into their products.

Photo CD opens up a number of possibilities. There are many photo libraries that supply colour and black and white photographs to magazines and book publishers week in, week out. Storing these images is a problem, but not if they are on CDs. Several hundred high quality colour images can be stored on a CD in a digital format that will never degrade. When a company places an order for a picture a photo library using Photo CDs would not need to make a print and then post it to the customer. The digital images could be transferred down a telephone line, using a computer modem, to the magazine or book publisher at the end of the line. It is a fast, efficient and cost effective process. But this scenario could be taken a step further. Instead of selling one photograph to a magazine the library could sell a CD full of images, ranging from pictures of cars to the latest super-model. Any image can be stored on a CD (see Figures 9.1 and 9.2).

Figure 9.1 A picture of Stonehenge saved as a Photo CD file

Photo CD lends itself perfectly to this type of business use and there are companies around the world experimenting with this. Corel is a Canadian software company which makes Windows drawing packages. In 1993 the company decided to make a move into the Photo CD world with a product range of 100 CDs containing high quality images. Around 100 images are stored on each CD which costs £80. An initial £80 fee allows a magazine to use any image as many times as it wants. The CDs include pictures of cars, World War II fighter aircraft, the arctic, wild animals and a host of other subjects. It is a very cheap way of collecting images for use in books and magazines.

**Figure 9.2 Another Photo CD image – this time a vintage World War II aircraft**

However, the publishing world is not the only place where these images can be used. In earlier chapters we have talked about business presentation graphics packages and the electronic replacement for overhead transparencies. Photo CD images can also be used to add a more professional edge to a slide presentation. A public relations office of a major corporation, such as ICI or Boeing, is constantly collecting photographic materials relating to its company. A Photo CD collection of images could easily be mass produced and distributed to staff for use in their business presentations.

Education is another area that can benefit from CD and Photo CD. Teachers are always using photographic materials to help students with the learning process. Again Photo CD can be used for various presentations a teacher would need to make. But more of teaching and multimedia later.

---

# CD-I

CD technology was invented by Sony and Philips. Between them the companies own just about every patent you would ever care to mention pertaining to CD. A few years ago the companies, mainly pushed by Philips, launched a technology called Compact Disc-Interactive (CD-I), a quantum leap forward in CD technology.

CD-I is a brilliant technology that was badly marketed and has unfortunately failed to make a big impact – yet. There are moves to bring CD-I and the PC CD-ROM formats closer together and it may yet be possible for Philips to make CD-I a success.

The consumer marketplace has always been the target of CD-I and as it stands there is nothing that can touch this clever piece of hardware. A standard audio CD player has been integrated into a matt black box, no larger than a standard VCR, and mixed with all the major components of a computer: memory and graphics. It is available for around £300. Once plugged into a TV set the CD-I player can be used to show games, education, electronic books, and much more. All the very best of multimedia is mixed together on CDs and sold for £30–£50.

The speed of a CD-I system is impressive. For example, one of the most talked about PC games, is Virgin's *The 7th Guest*. On even the very fastest of PCs – probably costing well over £1500 – this game runs sluggishly. But on a CD-I system this game is really fast. Why? Because CD-I is built from the ground up as a multimedia tool and not bolted together as an afterthought like the PC.

There is a lot of development work going on around CD-I and perhaps one of the most significant events was the release of Philips' £150 Full Motion Video (FMV) add-on box for CD-I. When this is bolted in – bringing the total system cost to £450 – the CD-I system turns into a low-cost digital laserdisc system.

Movie producers like Paramount have worked with Philips to take movies like *The Hunt for Red October* and *Star Trek VI: The Undiscovered Country* and put them onto a standard CD. Digitally recorded these £15 movies can be played on a CD-I system, fitted with a FMV module, and watched on a TV set. The picture quality is superb, better than VHS quality but not as advanced as laserdisc. But where CD-I movies score over VHS cassettes is in their control.

As the image is recorded digitally on the CD every frame of a movie is indexed. This means that a user has complete control over the movie. If you want to go to 23 minutes and 15 seconds into the movie the CD-I system will do so immediately.

It is this control that makes CD-I and its ilk a major attraction to the computer industry. Imagine an interactive game where a player is given a variety of options. Perform one task and the game has ending A, another task gives you ending B and so on.

If you then take this interactivity and add it to multimedia in the business or education world the whole technology comes alive. Imagine an interactive presentation in a history classroom where children are allowed to suggest different battle tactics at Waterloo or Trafalgar. Napoleon has a chance to win for a change and Lord Nelson manages to sidestep a bullet.

The same goes for an interactive shopping kiosk. A clothes shop could demonstrate its latest dresses from the catwalk of Paris. The software could be programmed so that a potential buyer can change the shoes, hat, colour, size and so on in order to see if the dress is really what they want.

## —— Other CD developments ——

Millions of bytes of information are needed to make this sort of interactive technology come alive and CD-ROM is the answer. Although only 600 MB of information can physically be stored on a CD, computer systems these days use what is known as a jukebox to give access to several CDs. Such a storage unit works in the same way as the old record-based jukebox used in many of today's pubs and clubs.

Education is a real winner when it comes to multimedia and CD. The whole education system could be completely re-engineered in order to give children access to better information. If a classroom has a network of computers all linked together then a single CD-based electronic book can be used by several or all of the children. The beauty of this is that a single CD can hold tens of thousands of simple text pages. The entire works of William Shakespeare can be stored on a CD with lots of space left over. But imagine a CD where the works of Shakespeare, in its simple form, are narrated by a famous actor, such as Sir John Geilgud or Patrick Stewart. Then add colour images, animations or video clips and the words come alive. Such CDs could have great educational value.

The CD is the future of PC storage as we know it. Software houses like Microsoft, Lotus, Borland and any other big business software supplier all want to replace magnetic disks as a means of distribution in favour of the CD. Simple market forces will make the hardware suppliers ship a CD-ROM drive as standard.

Software Publishing Corporation (SPC) is a large supplier of specialist graphics packages to professional users. The company has teamed up with Philips to offer its Harvard Graphics presentation graphics package on a CD bundled with a Philips CD-ROM drive. The company wants to move all of its software distribution onto CD. Instead of selling a set of floppy discs for every application sold, it plans to put its entire software collection onto one single CD and sell it to its customers. SPC then plans to sell its customers a code that unlocks more and more of the software on the CD as the customer pays more money. For example, the customer can pay £399 for Harvard Graphics and later on decide to pay another £150 to unlock some of SPC's image files also stored on the disk. A little later more images may be needed so another £150 is paid. The process is continued for as long as the customer is willing to keep paying. For SPC the benefits are clear: massively reduced manufacturing costs and significant ease when it comes to distributing software. The idea of several products on a single CD is also convenient for the retailer.

In addition to saving manufacturing costs the idea of CD-based business software can also negate the need for paper manuals. Software manufacturers can give their customers electronic manuals that can be accessed from within applications. They can also add multimedia tutorials to CDs which act as in-depth guides to the software.

The future of software distribution and use is definitely CD-based. Over the next few years a CD-ROM player will become an invaluable accessory.

# 10

# MINI REVIEWS OF
—   MULTIMEDIA   —
# SOFTWARE

To show how software companies are taking advantage of multimedia to engender a sense of 'electronic life' into books and databases this chapter will look at just a few of the many programs on the market. I have not attempted to cover the many every-day business applications that are now being transferred to the CD format. Prices of CDs range wildly from under £10 to well over £100, depending on the type of information contained on them. Unfortunately, it is not possible to discuss the merits of every multimedia application on the market so apologies to those that did not make it into the final batch looked at. Some approximate prices at the time of writing are given, but prices can vary considerably.

**Dinosaurs**
*Microsoft* (£35)

The child in each and every one of us has a love of the long dead dinosaur. Microsoft perfectly timed its launch of a multimedia guide to the fossilised world of Tyranosaurus Rex and Stegasaurus to coincide with the interest in the subject generated by Steven Spielberg's film *Jurassic Park*.

The start up screen of this CD offers a number of options including a guided tour of of the various dinosaur periods, including the now famous Jurassic time zone, and several dinosaur movies. These include *The Hunt* and *Young Dinosaurs*, and have been put together – at some cost to Microsoft – using Video for Windows.

Microsoft has put a great deal of work in this CD and has developed a superb product. As a teaching tool for a school child *Dinosaurs* would be invaluable and is a perfect demonstration of how to combine stereo sound, high quality images, text information and motion video sequences (Figure 10.1).

**Figure 10.1 Microsoft *Dinosaurs***

## The 7th Guest
*Virgin Software* (£70)

This adventure game is the ultimate in multimedia fun. It uses high resolution colour images to depict the goings on in a haunted house. Due to the complexity of these images *The 7th Guest* actually ships on two CDs – that's 1200 MB of data.

Whoever created these games obviously wanted to make a statement about the future direction of game playing. An example of the resources needed to play this game can be realised by number of tests performed before the game installs. First the speed of the CD-ROM drive the game will run from is tested, to make sure that a data transfer rate of over 150 KB per second can be achieved, and then the redrawing speed of the graphics card displaying it is checked to make sure that animations and sound effects can be properly synchronised.

*The 7th Guest* is a major leap forward in the quality of game playing. Unfortunately, the game lacks a level of playability. The main emphasis of the game is to discover the wicked secret of the house by completing a variety of complex tests located throughout the house.

The problem is that in making the game fantastic to look at the playability has been restricted. This no way limits its value for money. Immense pleasure can be had just from the graphics. Again Video for Windows has been used to make the game even more realistic and digitised speech from professional actors enhances the ambience.

Don't be too excited about the game play, it is incredibly difficult, but if you want to see how multimedia can be used to enhance games this is just the business.

### Cinemania '94
*Microsoft* (£35)

Any movie buff should really enjoy this CD-based guide to the world of high technology special effects, famous actors and classic movies. *Cinemania* brings together the movie knowledge of several American film publications:

> *Leonard Maltin's Movie and Video Guide*
> *5001 Nights At The Movies*
> *The Film Encyclopedia*
> *Roger Ebert's Video Companion*
> *The Motion Picture Guide Annual*
> and *The Film Glossary*

The program is neatly presented and comes complete with audio clips, musical scores, still images from several of the films and detailed biographies of actors, directors and producers. Detailed texts from the movies are also included (Figure 10.2).

All the latest movies are included on this CD-based guide and a fairly fast search engine allows a word or sentence to be searched for. A 'hit' list is then presented from which a number of options can be chosen.

For example, when I searched for Stallone the program came back with 77 occasions where the word/name Stallone was mentioned. By double-clicking on the name of a movie Stallone acted in, such as *First Blood*, I was able to pull out a complete guide to this movie, including cast, length of movie, grade out of five, other famous actors in the film and so on. I could also look at details of other films, a biography of the actor and a list of some of his earlier movies.

**Figure 10.2  Microsoft *Cinemania***

The search engine at the heart of Microsoft's movie CD is fast and flexible. A user can create a plethora of customised search routines to extract the information they require. A well written Help function guides you around the software, which is just as well because *Cinemania* ships without any manuals. Everything you need to know is stored on the CD. All you have to do is look for it.

### Art Gallery
*Microsoft* (£35)

Bill Gates, the chairman of Microsoft, is a great lover of classical art. In his home in Seattle, USA, he has electronic picture frames which can display whatever great work of art he wants to look at. Every morning he can wake up to Michelangelo, Raphael, or Degas.

Now you can experience classical works of art on *Art Gallery*. A richly put together CD, this program is in itself a 'work of art'.

The program opens by offering a number of picture options:

    Artists' lives
    Historical atlas
    Picture types

General reference
and Guided tours

The images stored on the CD are taken from the historical collection held in the National Gallery, London. Founded in 1824 the National Gallery is situated in Trafalgar Square and holds pictures from Western Europe dated from the 13th Century to the early 20th Century.

The Artists' lives option offers an A–Z of painters and is very complete in its listings. The CD includes everyone from Raphael whom we have all heard of to the likes of Mabuse, a Dutch painter who was active around 1503. Although he is not a well known painter, when you see his paintings stored on this Microsoft CD you are presented with beautiful pictures as complete as those of any great master (Figure 10.3).

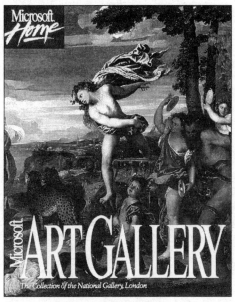

**Figure 10.3 Microsoft Art Gallery**

## Speed
*Guildsoft* (£307)

US software house Knowledge Adventure is a past master at piecing together very competent multimedia packages and *Speed* is a fast action computer-based ride into the world of fast moving cars, aircraft, people and animals.

The product is based around a 30 minute video, created by MacGillvray-Freeman, which is very well edited and remarkably informative. At any point during the video clip you can stop the action and jump into exactly what is happening and why.

The material used within *Speed* is well put together with high quality video clips and superb stereo sound effects. The only real problem is the clumsy menu system which leaves a lot to be desired. But if you concentrate on the images and sound at hand then you soon forget the menu problem.

Children of all ages will love this application, as will all adults. One of the most amusing ideas postulated by the software is why Albert Einstein, one of the world's greatest mathematicians, believed that the fastest thing in the Universe may not be light. He believed that the human imagination may well be faster.

The software is available on both CD and 3.5 inch high density floppy discs.

### 3-D Dinosaur Adventure
*Guildsoft* (£60)

This is the first CD-based multimedia application I have ever used that came with a pair of 3-D glasses. Earlier we mentioned the Microsoft *Dinosaurs* CD which is an amazing encyclopedia of facts about the long dead giants that once ruled the earth. This CD is not packed with as many facts but is a lot more fun.

On the CD version come 30 full colour, high resolution video clips complete with stereo digital sound effects. The floppy disk version comes with a mere six. The movies are a treat and well worth watching. But turn the volume control down on your sound card or you will frighten the neighbours.

Knowledge Adventure has put a lot of effort into the quality of these colour video clips and the fact that they are in 3-D is pretty effective. Normally those dreadful red and green spectacles don't work but with the videos included on the CD the image really comes to life.

In addition to the videos in *3-D Dinosaur* the software comes with several mini-adventures located inside the Virtual Reality Dinosaur Theme Park. You can take the Triassic Tour, Journey through the Jurassic Jungle or Creep Around the Cretaceous Corner. Inside each tour is a variety of animated dinosaurs, such as the towering torvosaurs and soaring pteranodons.

Once bored with the videos and mini-adventures you can delve into the Dino Encyclopedia. A multitude of questions will be answered: Where did dinosaurs come from? What did they eat? Which was the biggest? How small was the smallest?

Children will love the multimedia delight of *3-D Dinosaur* with the section that allows them to make their own prehistoric terror. All they have to do is pick a body and then add a pattern. You could quite easily end up with a wood-panelled Stegosaurus or gold-plated Parasaurolophus.

The best part of the CD is the Dino Museum which makes excellent use of the 3-D glasses. This is the ultimate exhibition of dinosaurs and is an amazing visual experience.

### King James Bible
*Guildsoft*

Software Marketing Corporation has attempted to make religious education a little more enjoyable by putting the King James edition of the Bible on a CD.

The application comes to life with a mixture of classic art, photographs, maps and timelines depicting exactly when the claimed events of the Bible occurred. A powerful search engine can be employed to search the Bible for a single word or string of words in a matter of seconds.

A quiz is also included in order to test your knowledge of biblical events. There are over 100 images, from the great masters and from actual sites in the Holy Land, included on the CD. Maps and journeys included depict the travels of people such as Moses, as well as the Exodus, the Promised Land and David's Kingdom.

A history of the Bible is included with information taken from the Pentateuch, the Dead Sea Scrolls and Modern Translations.

### The Collection: People
*Hulton Deutsch* (£350)

This is a wonderful CD if you are interested in famous people. It is in effect, a picture library with 10 000 images of 4000 famous people. Searches can be performed on topic, name, keyword or photographer.

However, many may consider the price a little too high, especially as all the images remain the property of Hulton Deutsch, so you have to pay a fee if you want to use any of them for publication.

## Undersea Adventure
*Guildsoft* (£30)

Like space and dinosaurs the mystery of the world's oceans interests children and adults alike. Knowledge Adventure has put together an amazing guide to the secrets of the sea with its *Undersea Adventure*.

The software gives you a front row seat from which you can watch whales breeching, sharks attacking, dolphins playing and a myriad of other fascinating oceanic spectacles. The CD comes complete with a 3D Zoomscape which allows you to enter the halls of a virtual aquarium.

Once inside you can play the Who Am I? game which teaches you the difference between a hump back whale, sperm whale and blue whale. There is even a Seacology Lab which allows you electronically to peel away the skin of a sea creature to examine its muscles and circulatory system. A host of text messages provides an interesting insight to how many of the oceans' giant animals live, breath and reproduce.

What exactly does a Great White Shark like to eat for breakfast? You, me or another shark? The answers lie hidden in *Undersea Adventure*.

## Clinton: Portrait of Victory
*Warner New Media*

For those keen on political figures, this one is a photographic tour of Clinton's rise to fame and fortune. Love him or hate him he is one of the most powerful men in history and this CD hides nothing. The disk is dual format, both Mac and PC, and covers President Clinton's career from its beginnings through the political campaign to power.

## The Animals!
*Software Toolworks*

*The Animals!* is a guided tour of the San Diego Zoo. It is a marvellous adventure for children and adults to learn about a wide number of animals – everything from a donkey to a leopard. It uses high quality still images, audio clips, motion video and rich text as a teaching tool. The software is easy to use and well equipped for children to learn a lot about the world they live in and the animals that dwell in it.

## Changing Times
*The Times Network Supplement*

This is a compilation of reports and pictures from *The Times* and *Sunday Times* newspapers over the last 200 years. World events can be found from a timeline menu or specific topics can be searched for through the database. Anyone interested in history will find this a fascinating collection, and the ability to search for people, places or events and browse through the picture library is an enthralling way to learn more about the world's history for both adults and children.

## Just Fonts
*ERC Computer Services*

Storing fonts can eat away huge chunks of your hard disk space, and anyone who likes experimenting with fonts will find that they will want access to the fonts easily, but may not use them often enough to warrant the loss of storage space. CD is the perfect medium for storing fonts.

This disk offers over 250 Adobe Type 1 and TrueType fonts for a moderate price. A viewer is included so that you can browse through the collection before installing the one you desire. There are the weird and wonderful fonts included on this CD, so there is bound to be something to satisfy everyone.

## Interactive Old Testament
*CD Express*

This CD offers poetry, stories and fables from the Old Testament. You choose the topics you are interested in from stone tablets which hold the menu options. Together with the stories, there is geography of the area, the politics of the time, and works of art from the period. Surprisingly, different religions are compared in a completely unbiased and very effective way. Examples of music from the time are supplied in MIDI format, and a range of narrated stories is provided for the younger audience.

## Global Explorer
*Unica*

I have always been disappointed by computer atlases in the past, and so I faced this CD with deep scepticism. It proved to be better than I had imagined, but was still not perfect.

*Global Explorer* displays a global map into which you can dive, zooming in on the areas of interest. This package did provide much more detail than I have seen on other similar floppy-disk-based programs, allowing you to zoom right in on cities, and see the road layouts of major highways.

However, don't jump to any conclusions. This is not a road atlas, and is not designed to show you the way from 79 London Road to 83 Mountford Crescent. It doesn't mark every town and village, but you could see the general route from city to city.

The other aim of the package is to provide information on countries, and some cities. It is limited in some areas, but still contains a lot of useful facts.

## Creepy Crawlies
*Media Design Interactive (MDI)*

Many people are scared stiff of tiny spiders. It's amazing just how frightened people are and this CD looks into why we should not be afraid. Media Design Interactive is a seasoned producer of multimedia software and has created a beautiful product with *Creepy Crawlies* (Figure 10.4).

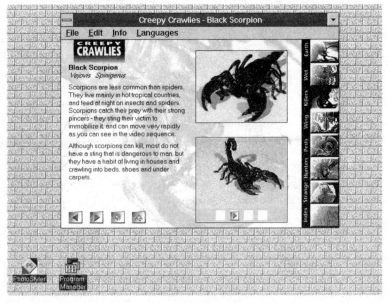

**Figure 10.4  A video nasty – *Creepy Crawlies***

The program mixes video clips of an average quality with digital speech – speech which becomes rather annoying after while – and text and colour images. The information presented is interesting and very educational.

### Introduction to Classical Music
*Unica* (£45)

This is a must for any Windows user interested in classical music. On launching the program, you are greeted with the *Four Seasons* and the menu. There are several ways of wandering through the information on the CD. A timeline shows when musical pieces were written, and an index lets you look up a particular work. Complete musical works are not supplied, but rather a couple of minutes of each piece of music along with background information on the composer and their picture. Each major composer is represented, along with many less well known.

The presentation on this CD is excellent. Once a piece of music has been selected to play, the program takes you to the auditorium where an orchestra is warming up in the background. The conductor calls the musicians to order, and the performance begins.

### Legend of Kyranda
*Virgin Games* (£37)

This is the first in a series of fantasy playing adventures known as *Fables and Fiends*. This is an adventure game in which the once magnificent castle of Kyranda has fallen under the wicked spell of the evil jester Malcolm. He holds the most powerful magical gemstone, the Kyragem. Your parents have been killed by the jester, and your grandfather has been turned to stone. Your job is to capture the maniac before he destroys the forest. This is a beautiful game in which every character speaks . If you like adventure games, then this is just one of Virgin's excellent selection in this area.

### The Brontë Sisters
*Nimbus* (£37)

The works of the Brontë Sisters have given many hours of pleasure. This CD provides a wonderful insight into the history of the Brontë novels, with a collection of illustrations by the Brontës, and photographs of the Sixty Treasures of the Brontë Parsonage Museum.

Making use of the multimedia capabilities, Nimbus has included spoken passages, biographies of the Brontës, and introductions to their novels. This would prove to be invaluable to any student studying their works. The complete novels provided include *Jane Eyre, Agnes Grey, The Tenant of Wildfell Hall* and *Wuthering Heights.*

## Deep Voyage
*Aris Entertainment*

From shipwrecks and hidden caves to deep and uncharted waters, watch plant and animal life come alive before your eyes. *Deep Voyage* is an underwater adventure that includes 100 photographic images in TIFF, BMP and PCX formats, 100 audio clips in WAV format and 25 underwater action videos. All clips are royalty free.

## So Much Shareware Two
*Unica*

This is just one of a host of CDs on the market full of shareware programs. This one contains over 600MB of recent software. Nothing on this disc is older than 1990 and most programs are dated 1992. An easy to use menu and help system make this simple to use. The CD is packed with Windows programs, MIDI sound files, and GIF pictures.

Games included are: *Tetris, Deathwatch, Wolfenstein* and *Jill of the Jungle*, as well as playable demos of *Falcon 3, Indiana Jones and the Last Crusade, Lemmings, Rick Dangerous 2* and *Prince of Persia.*

## World War II Archives
*Attica Cybernetics* (£149)

Although it is not cheap, the quality and information contained on this CD make it well worth the price. Hundreds of photos bring to life the horrific reality of World War II. There are only 16 film clips, but they are of excellent quality, and last for two to three minutes. You can look up the events of the war from a text-based timeline or delve into the database of art, sound and text.

## Dune
*Virgin Games*

The game of the famous David Lynch science-fiction film is now available on CD-ROM. In a strategy-based adventure set on the hellish desert planet of Arakis, Paul Atreides finds himself alone against the Harkonnen Empire. Both want Spice – the most powerful substance in the universe. As Paul Atreides, you must make friends with the Fremen to mine Spice and defend the Palace. The CD features astounding footage from the motion film, a slick CD soundtrack and crystal clear sampled speech with subtitles. It is an excellent game.

## The KGB/CIA World Factbook
*Compton's NewMedia*

'No one can be expected to know it all. That's why the members of the world's top spy agencies, the KGB and CIA, would never be caught without their special issue factbooks.' Well at least that's what Compton's claim. This CD is supposed to contain all the information that these sources hold. Topics covered on the disk include government statistics, economics, political and diplomatic protocol, industry and the environment, geography, treaties, trade, and drug traffic. I don't know that you'll be ready to become a world spy after looking through this CD, but it is full of fascinating information. You can find statistics for more than 250 countries and territories worldwide.

## Build and Race Motor Stars
*Revell*

From Revell, usually better known for its models than its software comes a new concept in gaming. *Motor Stars* combines a multimedia game with playing perfect modelling. This is a racing game featuring four of Europe's best racing machines from Porsche, Lamborghini, Bugati and Nazca. A detailed plastic model kit for the Porsche 'Slant Nose' is also included.

# 11

# GLOSSARY OF MULTIMEDIA TERMS

The idea of this glossary is to explain what all those lovely and obscure technical words mean. Most of the terms used in this book are covered, but do not use the glossary only to look up words. Browsing through it will help you understand the technology behind multimedia.

**Aliasing**
There are several explanations of aliasing but the simplest is that it is a visual effect, normally jagged, which is caused by the large pixels in a low resolution display. The effect is most noticible on lines that are not exactly vertical or horizontal.

**Anti-aliasing**
This is a computer technique to overcome the creation of jagged lines on a display. The graphics card compensates for the 'wonky' line by fooling the human eye. For example, consider a diagonal line made of white pixels which is surrounded on both sides by black pixels. Anti-aliasing will change the white pixels at the edge of the line into grey pixels which makes the human eye resolve the combination of black, white and grey into a straight line.

**Analogue**
An analogue signal has a value that is continuously variable. The data held by an analogue signal is very accurate, but the information is difficult to process and store. See *Digital* for the opposite to analogue.

**Aspect ratio**
This is the ratio between width and height. We are all used to watching TVs with an aspect ratio of 4:3 (that is four units across by three units high). Widescreen TVs, which attempt to simulate a cinema screen, have an aspect ratio of 16:9 (sixteen units across by nine high). With the majority of video capture systems, such as Intel SmartVideo and Videologic Captivator, the aspect ratio can be

altered, but remember that this will often distort the image. Have a try and see.

## AT

Advanced Technology. The IBM personal computer based on the 80286 chip was called the PC-AT. It has since been superseded by the 386, 486 and Pentium processors, all of which remain compatible with the original PC-AT.

## AUTOEXEC.BAT

This is the name of a start up file on the PC. This file contains an AUTOmatically EXECuted BATch of commands, hence the name. The commands held in this file must be executed as soon as the machine is started in order to run any further software programs. The AUTOEXEC.BAT is the second file to be executed on starting the PC.

## AVI

The abbreviation for audio/video interleaved. This is the file format that Microsoft Video for Windows uses to store video clips. See Chapter 7.

## Bandwidth

The amount of data that can be carried from one part of a computer transmitted in a set period of time.

## Betamax

An ill-fated video tape format that was successful in Japan but failed in Europe.

## BIOS

Binary Input Output System. This is the information and instructions necessary for a PC to perform basic functions on first being turned on. It is held on a read only memory (ROM) chip and allows the main processor to communicate with other parts of the computer and run basic diagnostics.

## Bit

Basically the smallest unit in a computer's binary system. A bit can have one of two possible values, 0 or 1, which depicts whether something is switched off or on.

## Bitmap

The name given to a graphic which is displayed using bitmapping. A bitmapped image is displayed by converting it into a number of dots. These dots are then transferred onto a grid by the computer which acts as a map to display the image as it should be.

### Boot
To turn the computer on.

### Bus
The route through which components in the computer communicate with each other.

### Byte

A byte is the smallest addressable unit of a computer's memory, and each byte consists of eight bits. In more powerful computers bytes can be processed in multiples of 8, 16, 32 or 64 bits.

### Cache
An area in memory which is temporary allocated to hold frequently used specific information from the hard disk. This enables the computer to access the information quicker than if it was pulled from the hard disk every single time it was needed.

### CAV
Constant angular velocity. Video disks spin at a constant speed and support rapid, frame accurate access to the digital material on the disk. The most common use is for interactive video with each disk capable of storing 30 minutes of video per side plus two audio channels. Compare with CLV.

### CD
Compact disk. A digital data storage medium that uses 12 centimetre reflective optical disks from which data is read by a laser. This device now dominates the music world and is steadily encroaching into the mainstream computer arena. CD is now the common abreviation for CD-DA.

### CD-DA
Compact disk – digital audio. Every CD sold in a high street store is recorded to this standard – 44.1 kHz 16-bit PCM.

### CD-I
Compact disk interactive. Invented by Philips and Sony, CD-I is a digital storage medium that allows users to interact with video, still images, audio, digital graphics and text on the same CD. CD-I comes in three classes:

- Class A is 37.8 kHz, 8-bit ADPCM (a space saving over PCM of 2:1). This equates to long play record quality.

- Class B is 37.8 kHz, 4-bit ADPCM (a space saving over PCM of 4:1). This equates to FM radio quality.

- Class C is 18.9 kHz, 4-bit ADPCM (a space saving over PCM of 4:1). This equates to AM radio quality.

### CD-ROM
Compact disk-read only memory. A generic offspring of CD-DA, CD-ROMs are read-only optical disks. Information is permanently stamped onto the disks during manufacture and each disk can hold approximately 600 MB.

### CD-ROM/XA
Compact disk-read only memory / extended architecture. The coming together of CD-ROM storage and the digital music quality of CD-DA. CD-ROM/XA offers 600 MB of storage plus ADPCM audio, taken from the CD-I world which allows for the interleaving of sound and picture data for animation and sound synchronisation.

### CGA
Colour graphics adaptor. The first video card to allow graphics to be displayed on a PC screen. The maximum possible resolution would only show up to 600 × 200 pixels the screen. This standard is now obsolete, and the cards are no longer manufactured although software can still be bought that supports this display.

### Chrominance
The part of a video signal that carries hue and colour saturation. Chrominance is often abreviated to C or Chroma.

### CLV
Constant linear velocity. CLV disks assign a fixed track length to each frame or sector which means they operate faster when reading from the outside of the disk, and slower when reading from the inside. CLV is most common in the domestic world where laser disks need to store more information without the need for individual frame control offered by CAV disks. These disks offer 60 minutes of video per side plus two audio channels.

### Compact disk
See CD.

### Compact disk – digital audio
See CD-DA.

### Compact disk-Read Only Memory
See CD-ROM.

### Compact disk-Read Only Memory/Extended Architecture
See CD-ROM/XA.

### Composite Video
A video signal where the brightness, colour and synchronisation information of a picture are combined in one signal. The most common sources for composite video are VHS and Betamax video recorders, and the majority of camcorders.

### Compression
The translation of data into a much more compact form designed to ease storage or transmission.

### CONFIG.SYS
This file must be in the root directory of a hard disk and is used by the computer to configure the system to certain parameters every time it is switched on. Although a computer will operate without this file, most software requires certain commands to be present in the CONFIG.SYS file before it will run.

### Control panel
This icon is found in Microsoft Windows, and when activated opens a window holding all the basic configuration programs for Windows and the computer. It is from here that Windows lets you change the colour of your screen; control your mouse; set the date and time; and install and configure drivers.

In the Macintosh System 7, a folder holds separate control panels for each specific item.

### Co-processor
This is a companion to the main processor (CPU) and performs more specialised functions and calculations such as mathematical or graphical processing. This allows the CPU to run the whole system at maximum speed rather than slowing down for heavy calculations.

### CPU
Central Processing Unit. This is the chip around which the computer is based, i.e. 386, 486. It performs all major calculations necessary for the computer to work.

### Cut
This is a simple effect where a screen or image immediately

changes into another image without a transition effect.

## CVBS
See composite video.

## DAT
Digital audio tape. This is a high quality audio storage medium which uses a 48 kHz 16-bit PCM audio standard.

## Data rate
This is the speed at which information can be transferred and processed by your computer.

## Data transfer rate
This is the speed at which information can be moved from one point to another, be it within your computer, or externally across a network or down a phone line.

## Device driver
Small programs necessary for the computer to communicate with additional external or internal devices extra to the basic computer features.

## DIB
Device independent bitmap. This is an image file format supported by Video for Windows.

## Digital
Information is stored in a digital system with binary numbers (0 and 1). Digital data is more precise, consistent and manageable than analogue data which makes it the preferred choice for use in computer systems.

## Digital camera
A camera which stores images in a digital format, thereby making it simple to transfer the images to a computer.

## Digitising
This is the method by which an analogue signal, audio or video is captured by a computer and the information within it converted into 0s and 1s.

## Disk access
The process by which information is read from or written to a disk. Hard disk or floppy disk drive specifications often state a time for this process which enables users to determine how fast the drive accesses data. The peak disk access time can be affected by many

factors, and it is rare for a disk to achieve the manufacturer's quoted fastest access time.

**Disk controller**
This is the component within the computer that controls all the disk functions. There are both hard disk and floppy disk controllers.

**DPI**
Dots per inch. This is a measurement of picture quality either on screen or from a printer. An image, whether text or graphic is built up with dots. The larger the number the better, i.e. a 600 DPI printer will produce a sharper image than a 300 DPI printer.

**EGA**
Enhanced graphics adaptor. This was introduced in 1985 as a step up from CGA. It is capable of displaying 640 × 350 dots on the screen, and only 16 colours may be displayed on the screen at any one time from a palette of 64.

**EISA**
Extended industry standard architecture. This is a type of PC bus, that can transfer 32 bits of information at a time compared with 8 or 16 bits of data on a standard (ISA) PC. This not only means the computer can work faster, but it directly affects the speed with which the computer will talk to expansion cards that are added into it. While EISA computers will accept ISA cards, there is no performance gain, and in fact adding non-EISA cards to an EISA machine can slow the whole system down. However, many EISA cards are more expensive than their ISA counterparts, and so sometimes trade-offs have to be made.

**Extended memory**
Memory over the first 1024KB including the high memory area (HMA).

**Fade**
A special effect where video, graphics or audio can grow stronger (fade in) or weaker (fade out).

**Field**
A field is a set of scan lines that makes up one half of a video frame. Every other line of the image is put into the first field and all the intervening lines into the second. When displayed, these two fields are interlaced – or alternated line by line – in order to produce a complete picture or frame. The reason this interlacing model is used on broadcast images is so that low frame rates can be broadcast

without excessive flicker. With NTSC this is 30 frames (or 60 fields) every second, with PAL accounting for 25 frames (or 50 fields) every second.

**File format**
All software programs have their own way of creating and saving files. These are known as file formats. While file formats differ from package to package, and often from one version of software to another, there are a few common formats that most software programs support. It is becoming increasingly common for software programs to support the file formats of their large competitors, e.g. the word processing packages Word, WordPerfect and WordStar each support the others' file formats.

**File fragmentation**
The DOS operating system saves files to a disk by writing sector sized pieces of the file from memory into free sectors on the destination disk. Although the operating system attempts to write them as contiguous sectors this is not always possible. As a disk fills up files may become fragmented across a disk which impairs performance. Utilities like Norton Speed Disk can be used to move all of the fragments into one contiguous data sequence which will improve performance.

**Floppy disk (or diskette)**
The name given to any magnetic disk that is not fitted as an integral part of a computer. These disks are a thin, round, flat piece of Mylar and store magnetic fields. The most common floppy discs are $3^1/2$ inches and $5^1/4$ inches in size. The former are encased in a solid rigid plastic and are now the standard.

**Format**
Every disk (hard and floppy) must be formatted before it can be used to store information. Formatting a disk prepares it by magnetically marking out tracks and sectors in a kind of circular pattern. Once this is done a directory is created which will list the information held in each sector of the disk.

**Fractal**
A form of mathematic calculation defined by mathematician Benoit Mandelbrot to create complex graphical displays. The basis of fractals is that any portion of a complex fractal image has the same mathematical characteristics of the entire image. The process of identifying mathematical characteristics can help in the reduction

of file sizes especially when it comes to complex graphics and video files.

## Frame
The generic term denoted to each single, and complete picture in a video sequence. The number of frames displayed every second depends upon the television standard being used (see NTSC and PAL). PAL video is 25 FPS and NTSC is 30 FPS, compared with a movie which is 24 FPS.

## Frame dropping
There are times when a computer is capturing a video sequence that it fails to capture all of the frames. This is known as frame dropping. The technique can be implemented deliberately, when a PC's bandwidth is limited, or it can occur accidently when system performance fails.

## Frame rate
The speed at which a moving video sequence is updated every second. It is measured in frames per second, which is abbreviated to FPS.

## Full motion
A term commonly misused by most computer users. Full motion refers to a computer's ability to display, in real-time, the correct screen rate for PAL, NTSC or motion pictures. See also *Frame rate*.

## Gamma
The relationship between the voltage changes produced by a graphics card and the brightness changes that appear on a monitor because of them. Most computer monitors have different gamma characteristics to video and TV monitors.

## GIF
Graphics interchange format. This is a graphics format that compresses images for storage. Originally developed to make transferring graphics over networks easier, this file format is commonly used on bulletin boards, but not supported by all software packages.

## Greyscale
The tone of an image. Computer images are not just black and white (monochrome) or colour, they can also be grey. While monochrome images consist of only black or white dots, greyscale images are made up of different shades of grey dots. This makes for a much sharper image than plain monochrome. Greyscale is also

one version of TIFF, and it is possible to display and save an image in up to 256 greyscales.

**Hard disk**
A device that uses a magnetic head to read and write data onto platters that spin at high speed inside a sealed vacuum.

**Hi8 Video**
A low-cost video tape format with a 400 line horizontal resolution and Y/C input. Y/C is a separate input and output for luminance (Y) and chrominance (C) channels.

**Interlacing**
A technique used to double the vertical resolution of a broadcast image by broadcasting each individual image as two sets of alternating lines. This is achieved by drawing even numbered lines in one pass and odd-numbered in the next pass, which means the two consecutive fields draw a single image. TV pictures were developed this way to compensate for the low bandwidth restrictions on early TV signals. A low bandwidth normally offers a low frame rate and a low frame rate means a low scan rate which equates to a poor image quality. By splitting each frame into two fields the scan rate is effectively doubled, giving a more stable picture.

**Interlace flicker**
Interface flicker is only a worry with computer graphics because the high resolutions, often dispalyed as a single pixel line, will cause a screen flicker because they only appear in one field of the interlaced frame.

**ISA**
Industry standard architecture. This is the 16-bit replacement to the 8-bit bus, and is the standard architecture for the majority of PCs. It precedes the MCA and EISA buses, and will still accept 8-bit cards.

**JPEG**
Joint Photographics Experts Group, a joint sub committee of the International Telegraph and Telephone Consultative Committee and International Standards Organisation. It is also the abbreviation for a compression technique for continuous tone (real life, full colour) still images. JPEG is a symmetrical compression/decompression algorithm. This means that the method used to decompress an image is the exact reverse of the technique used to compress it, and takes the same time for both actions. JPEG uses what is known as a lossy algorithm. This is a compression

technique that loses information during the compression process. The greater the compression the greater the loss of information in a file.

## Kilobyte
A kilobyte consists of 1024 bytes of information.

## Lossless
A compression algorithm that does not lose information from a data file when it compresses it, but this type of algorithm has a low compression ratio.

## Lossy
An algorithm that is forced to lose information from a data file during the process of data compression. See JPEG.

## Luminance
The part of a video signal that contains all the information on brightness and contrast. Luma or Y are also names that Luminance is known by.

## Megabyte
One megabyte (MB) of memory or disk space, or 1,048,576 bytes.

## MCA
Micro channel architecture. Developed by IBM and brought to the market in 1987 in its PS/2 range of computers, MCA carries data at 32-bits rather than the 16-bit performance of ISA. MCA is an intelligent architecture in that it will automatically configure the system to work with expansion cards. However, MCA failed to sweep the market as IBM had hoped due to its lack of support for conventional ISA cards. MCA cards are still expensive, and only a handful of PC manufacturers have MCA machines.

## Megahertz
A measure of frequency. One hertz is one cycle per second. A frequency of 1 megahertz (MHz) means that for example, an electric current is oscillating at one million times per second. This measurement is used to state the speed of a processor, e.g. 25, 33, 50 and 66 MHz.

## Memory, conventional
DOS automatically uses the first 640KB of a PC's RAM to run programs in. This 640KB is referred to as conventional memory, as extra commands are required to recognise any additional memory that may be in a PC.

## MIPS

Millions of instructions per second. A measurement of how fast a computer performs its tasks.

## Monochrome

An image, whether it be on a screen or as a graphic to be scanned or printed, made up purely of black and white dots.

## Motherboard

The backbone of the computer. The CPU, the memory and all the basic circuitry of the computer are situated on this circuit board. Additional devices such as expansion boards, disk drives and ports link up to the motherboard.

## Mouse

A plastic device, external to the computer, which allows the user to control the pointer on the screen. Movements made by pushing the mouse across the desk correspond to the movement of the cursor across the screen. Buttons on the mouse make it possible to select commands and programs without using the keyboard.

## Multimedia

If you don't understand this term yet then this book has failed in its job. But just to recap, multimedia is the mixture of text, audio, graphics and video used to present and communicate information to an audience.

## Multitask

Performing more than one task at a time. This term is most often used when referring to operating systems. Unix, OS/2 and Windows NT are multitasking operating systems, in that they can command the computer to do many jobs at any one time. DOS can only perform one task at a time, although Windows 3.1 runs several applications concurrently by allocating each a set amount of processing time (time slicing).

## NTSC

The National Television Standards Committee (NTSC) is the video standard for colour TV used throughout North America, Japan and some South American countries. This TV standard differs to the UK's PAL standard in that the number of frames per second (30), lines displayed on a screen (525) and the method of encoding colour are different.

## Operating system

A software program that sits between the computer components and the software packages, such as a wordprocessor, that you want to use. DOS, OS/2, Windows NT, System 7 and Unix are all operating systems. They allow software packages to tell the computer what tasks it must perform. The industry is working towards allowing packages that are specific to one operating system to work with other systems.

### Optical disks
Disks that are written to and read from using light (laser).

### Overscan
An average TV can only display a given area of any video image. This is known as the 'safe area' and the technique known as overscanning scans the image beyond the limits of the safe area and therefore off the edge of a TV screen.

### Paint program
A software package that allows you to create bitmapped graphics files. Paint programs allow you to move areas of an image around on screen, change the colouring of an image, and draw new graphics on the screen.

### PAL
Phase Alternation Line. It is the colour TV broadcast standard for the UK. PAL displays 625 lines at a frame rate of 25 FPS.

### Palette
The colour palette is used to define the colours assigned to digital images and video sequences. Palettes depend upon the image captured and with an 8-bit image up to 256 colours can be assigned.

### PCM
Pulse Code Modulation, a technology used for converting analogue audio signals into digital values by sampling the analogue signal (at a rate twice that of the maximum signal frequency), and then a binary value is applied to the sample.

### .PCX
A file format for storing bitmapped graphic images on PCs. PCX files are supported by most graphics packages.

### Peripheral
A generic term given to any piece of equipment connected to a computer, such as a printer or scanner.

### Pixel
A screen image is made up of thousands of dots of light. Each dot

visible to the human eye is called a pixel. Each pixel is in turn made up of three different coloured dots which are not visible to the human eye. A screen resolution is measured in the number of pixels displayed; for example a VGA monitor will display 640 × 480 pixels.

## Port
A port is a socket for connecting an external device to the main computer.

## Processor
An electronic device (chip) made from silicon which performs numerous calculations at very high speed. A computer and all external devices are powered by processors.

## Program Manager
Program Manager is specific to Windows. It is the main window from which all other software packages and utility programs are accessed. Each program has its own icon, and similar programs are grouped together in windows inside the Program Manager.

## RAM
Random access memory. A computer's memory. It is important to distinguish between this and the hard disk. RAM chips inside the computer store information temporarily while the computer is switched on. As soon as the computer is turned off, the information in memory is lost unless it is stored on a disk. Conventional memory, upper memory, extended memory, expanded memory and HMA memory are all held in RAM chips. These types of memory only differ from each other by the way the computer accesses the RAM chips. The user is not normally aware of what is held in memory as this is handled automatically by the computer.

## RAM drive (or RAM disk)
A section of memory that has been specified to act as a temporary disk. It is assigned a drive letter, and displays a directory of the files held on it. It is possible to copy files to and from this drive, but any files held here will be lost when the machine is switched off.

## Resolution
The quality of an image whether it be printed or displayed on a screen. Resolution on screen is measured by the number of pixels being displayed, while the resolution of a printed image is measured by the number of dots printed per inch (DPI).

## RGB

Red, Green and Blue. An RGB video signal is made up of these three component parts. A computer's graphics card (VGA or SVGA) outputs a colour signal in this format.

## Scaling

The measures taken to limit automatically the amount of digital data to fit within a given bandwidth.

## SCSI

Small computer systems interface. A standard for connecting devices to a computer. It is most commonly used when adding a disk drive, scanner or CD-ROM player to a system. Most computers do not come with a SCSI port as standard, so require a SCSI expansion card. The benefit of this cabling device is its speed and the ability to link up to seven devices to the one card. This is done by connecting one device into the back of another (daisy chaining).

## Sound card

An expansion card that adds sound capabilities to a computer, allowing music or speech to be played through external speakers.

## SVGA

SuperVGA. A video resolution of 800 × 600 pixels.

## S-VHS

The Super-VHS format. This video cassette format uses the same half inch tape format as standard VHS tapes. However, the standard of the tape has been greatly improved over normal VHS tape and the electronics have been enhanced to give better video results. S-VHS has a resolution of over 400 lines and a bandwidth of 4.5 MHz, and outputs an S-Video signal.

## S-Video

Separate Video. This video signal standard has a Y/C format, or a separate channel for luminance (black and white) and for chrominance (colour) information. S-Video avoids a number of the problems associated with the composite (CVBS) video signal, such as low power and degradation, but is normally employed by only the more expensive VCR systems.

## Swap file

A file created on the hard disk by Windows where data files and parts of programs are stored when they are not being used by the current application. When Windows runs out of memory it uses the hard disk to store the information that would otherwise be held in memory. Although this does enable you to run programs that would otherwise refuse to run due to lack of memory, swapping information to disk does slow the system down enormously.

## SYSTEM.INI
A Windows configuration file that may be edited in a text editor.

## TIFF
Tagged image file format. A popular graphic file format.

## VCR
Video cassette recorder. An electronic device that records and plays back video signals that have been stored on removable tape cassettes.

## Video adaptor
An expansion card that determines what resolution and how fast you can display images on a monitor.

## Virtual memory
Simulation of RAM by using a computer's hard disk as if it were memory.

## VGA
An IBM graphics standard that was introduced when IBM launched its PS/2 desktop computer. It has the ability to display 256 colours at a resolution of 640 × 480 pixels.

## VHS
Video home standard. This is the tape size and standard used in video cassette recorders. The tapes have a 240 line resolution, and a 2.5 MHz bandwidth; they output a composite video signal.

## Wipe
A special effect that is designed to make one picture replace another by moving across the screen, in any one of a number of directions, to cover the former image.

## Video 8
In the camera world the VHS tape format is too large to make a camera truly portable. The 8mm video tape format is more compact and offers a slightly better picture quality than that of VHS.

## Voice recognition
The ability of a computer to recognise spoken words as commands.

## XGA
A video adaptor for IBM's range of PS/2 computers. It has a resolution of 1024 × 768 pixels with up to 65 000 different colours displayed on screen at a time.

## XT
Extended technology. The PC architecture based around an 8088 processor that preceded the AT architecture.

## Y
See *Luminance*.

## Y/C
A video format that carries a separate luminance (Y) and chrominance (C) information.

# 12

# – THE MPC STANDARD –

The computer industry has never been very good at setting standards. The old fashioned way of setting a standard in this industry was generally accomplished by the company with the biggest clout.

Microsoft has always been good at setting standards and a few years ago it got together with several other leading PC companies to formulate the Multimedia Personal Computer (MPC) standard. Any computer or software package that wanted to display the MPC logo had to match the specification defined by the companies that established MPC. At the time Microsoft and its allies set a minimum requirement for a PC in order for it to be classed as multimedia-based. Unfortunately, the initial specification was too low and failed miserably to offer a PC capable of supporting multimedia software. The initial draft did, however, serve a purpose in that it got the message out to both end users and suppliers that multimedia was on its way.

Now the specification has been revamped and this time it is much better. The basic MPC level II specification now requires a PC to be based around the 25 MHz 486SX microprocessor and come with 4 MB of memory, 160 MB hard disk drive, 16-bit sound card, 640 × 480 pixel VGA card, and double-speed CD-ROM drive with multisession support and small computer system interface (SCSI).

Now this basic specification is fine for playing a multimedia game or replaying a multimedia clip from a CD-ROM. It is a perfect as playback unit, but not as anything else. Even for this machine, a basic entry level model, 8 MB of memory is recommended, as well as a double-speed CD-ROM drive with XA audio capability and an accelerated video card with a resolution of 640 × 480 pixels displaying 65 536 colours.

The next step from the entry level station is the MPC Development Station. This needs to have a powerful processor, such as a 33 MHz 486 chip, and a minimum of 8 MB of memory, 200 MB plus of hard disk, 16-bit sound card, 640 × 480 or higher resolution video card,

14 in colour monitor and a double-speed, multisession CD with Photo CD capability.

The operating system that is supposed to run on both these machines is Windows, which will enable them to both be classed as MPC. Of course Windows is not the only operating system capable of running multimedia software.

The next MPC machine type is called the Enhanced Station which is based around a 66 MHz 486 chip with 16 MB of memory, 500 MB plus of hard disk, a 16-bit sound card, a minimum screen resolution of 800 × 600 pixels, 17 inch monitor, double-speed, multisession CD-ROM player with SCSI interface and Photo CD support, and a video capture board.

Microsoft jokingly quips that this sort of machine should be 'able to dim the lights' when it is turned on. As you can see from the specification this machine is close to the ones built in Chapter 8. Such a machine will run the Windows operating system, but also has the ability to run Windows NT software. NT is a 32-bit version of Windows 3.1 which is very powerful and ideal for running multimedia applications. This is a multi-tasking, multi-threaded operating system that can process several pieces of data at the same time; it can also run several applications at the same time.

Microsoft likes to recommend Windows NT as the platform for developing multimedia applications. Personally I disagree with this. Microsoft is desperate to make people accept Windows NT and to take it into the mainstream as a replacement for the more common 16-bit Windows 3.1. All you need as an operating system is Windows 3.1 or OS/2 2.1. Both these software packages are perfectly adequate for most multimedia application development work.

The MPC specification is currently adequate for today's multimedia requirements but like many things the course of time will change this. At the moment a Windows-based PC designed around an Intel 486SX is good enough to be given an MPC 2.0 label. This fine for now. However, the 486SX chip is simply not powerful enough for most multimedia applications. A full blown 486DX running at 33 or 50 MHz is more like it and as people find more new things to do with multimedia eventually the Pentium chip will become the entry level requirement.

The MPC standard is changing all the time to reflect the changes in the industry. At the moment only Intel-based PCs are supported by

MPC but in later years there is nothing to stop a PowerPC-based Apple Macintosh or a Digital Alpha machine from qualifying for an MPC label. We will just have to wait and see.

PowerPC is set to really make an impact over the next few years. The chip is very fast and therefore a superb workhorse for multimedia. Apple has always had a strong presence in the multimedia arena and has vowed to make PowerPC a success with this technology. With the System 7.1 operating system running on the PowerPC a large amount of existing multimedia software, designed to run on the old Macintosh computer, works unchanged. However, for PowerPC to really make an impact in the multimedia arena companies like Lotus, Microsoft, IBM, Videologic, Claris, Adobe, and many more need to convert their existing software and hardware to support PowerPC.

Alpha looks unlikely to support multimedia outside the world of Microsoft Windows NT. To date this is the only important desktop operating system to work with the Alpha chip.

The future appears rosy for multimedia but standards need to keep up with developments. The industry has gone so far down the road with the MPC standard and this has made it easy for people to buy software and hardware they know will be compatible with each other. But as multimedia matures and hardware becomes more powerful the MPC standard has to mature with it, and the MPC Council has to recognise that there is more to life than Intel-based PCs running Windows software. Just because there are countless millions of people running Windows does not mean that this piece of software is the best operating system for running multimedia. Over the next few years rivals to Windows will continue to appear and who knows, another standard may develop.